# THE OPPOSITE OF COMBAT

# THE OPPOSITE OF COMBAT

A Parents' Guide for Teaching Siblings How to Collaborate and Solve Their Own Conflicts

## SUSAN NORTH

GoodMedia Press

An imprint of goodmedia communications, llc

25 Highland Park Village, 100-810

Dallas, Texas 75205

www.GoodMediaPress.com

Cover design by Lindsey Bailey

Book design by GoodMedia Press

The text in this book is set in Palatino.

Manufactured in the United States of America

Names: North, Susan, 1948-, author.

Title: The Opposite of combat : a parents' guide for teaching siblings how to collaborate and solve their own conflicts / Susan North.

Description: Includes bibliographical references and index. | Dallas, Tx: GoodMedia Press, 2019.

Identifiers: LCCN 2019945912 | ISBN 978-1-7327046-5-7 (pbk.) | 978-1-7327046-6-4 (ebook)

Subjects: LCSH Parenting. | Child rearing. | Brothers and sisters. | Sibling rivalry. | Families. | Parent and child. | Children—Family relationships. | Social interaction in children. | Interpersonal relations in children. | Interpersonal conflict. | Behavior modification. | Change (Psychology) | BISAC FAMILY & RELATIONSHIPS / Parenting / General | FAMILY & RELATIONSHIPS / Siblings

Classification: LCC HQ755.8 .N676 2019 | DDC 649/.1--dc23

*This book is lovingly dedicated to my sister, Bobbie North*
*And to the memory of our parents, Collette and Ed North*

# CONTENTS

# PREFACE
## Halley's Comet

In early 1986, my son was five years old and my daughter was three. For the second time in the twentieth century, Halley's Comet was making its regular appearance. I was captivated by the idea that, if my children were lucky enough to live into their seventies, they would experience this event twice in their lives. Though they were quite young, I was determined that they experience this spectacle, and I wanted it to be memorable for them.

We made plans with some friends to meet in the mountains near our home late one night. I made hot cocoa, and we woke the kids around midnight. We bundled them into the car and drove up the steep mountain through dense fog. Several times, we were tempted to turn back. It looked hopeless — was this going to be a terrible disappointment? Then, just as we rounded the last curve before the road opened up onto a small mountaintop plain, the clouds parted. It was magical. Above us shone a million stars, and we did indeed see the comet and its misty trail.

We snuggled back into the car and enjoyed our cocoa. Driving home, we talked about what we had seen. Inspired by the comet's majesty as well as the coziness of that shared family experience, I told the kids, "When you are both old, in about 75 years, Halley's

Comet will return, and you'll be able to see it again. I hope the two of you will make a plan to meet and see it together. Will you do that for me?" I could see two sleepy heads in the rearview mirror.

"Promise?"

"Yes, Mom."

Why was that so important to me? Let's set aside the absurdity of trying to forge a 75-year contract with a dozing preschooler; my wish was, of course, largely symbolic. Isn't it natural for parents to hope that our children will grow up to be friends and to "be there" for one another long after we're gone? Amidst all the bickering and competing for time and attention and resources that accompany the raising of siblings, this often looks like a futile hope. We all know adult siblings who are indifferent to one another, even pairs who are locked in jealous or resentful turmoil. Worse still, some are estranged. But we also know adult siblings who are good friends, whose lives are lovingly entwined and mutually enriching. How does that happen? Certainly some of it is pure luck — the alchemy of temperament and circumstance. But I like to think that parenting can play a role.

Part of what motivated me to write this book is the desire to seek and share ways to manage sibling conflict in a way that helps the young family have a more bearable day-to-day existence. I'm also moved by the conviction that skillful handling of siblings' conflict in the early years lays the groundwork for a sound relationship between those same siblings when they are adults.

And I hope I'm not being grandiose in believing that children whose conflicts are acknowledged and managed in an emotionally healthy way can grow up to be better citizens of the world.

# INTRODUCTION

I was raised in the fifties, before "parent" was a verb. Parent was something you were, not something you did. In the time I've been alive, the job of childrearing has been scrutinized, reviewed, re-thought, challenged, tweaked, and torqued as never before. Today's parents are overwhelmed with information and advice. Once confined to books and magazines, this avalanche of guidance now also tumbles upon us through ever more ingenious technologies and media. So why another book? Why *this* book?

As a young mom, I found parenting books both engaging and exasperating. They touched an eager chord, but they sometimes seemed incompatible with who I was. I could find competing opinions on nearly every topic. The cynic in me noted that if there were so many experts, perhaps if I just kept reading I would eventually find validation for what I was already believing and doing. My inner non-cynic kept browsing, adding this and that to my parenting repertoire. In truth, I was honing my belief system — and my practice — all the while. I still am.

I always tell my parenting classes, "Your child is your primary textbook. Careful and attentive observation will tell you most of what you need to know. *You* are the world's greatest living expert about the person(s) you are raising." I offer up this book in that spirit. It's merely a resource, not an instruction manual or collection of recipes for good parenting — heaven forbid! In it, I invite you to think about conflict in perhaps a new way and to try, if you like, to fit some techniques that I think are useful into the life you are already living and the parenting you are already doing.

There are wonderful parenting books that address the matter of raising siblings (see Annotated Bibliography at the end of this book) and most of them encourage us to let kids work it out. But most young children lack the language, self-control, and patience to do this independently, and I've found that there's a scarcity of specific, detailed information about how parents might *facilitate the process from a neutral position* — which is to say, *mediate*.

Although I had studied child development and worked in the field, it wasn't until I had kids of my own that I got to witness these kinds of facilitations. My own two kids attended Pacific Oaks Children's School in Pasadena, where for the first time I observed adults guiding children through conflicts in such a way that the kids resolved matters themselves. I also trained with Magda Gerber of RIE (Resources for Infant Educarers) where I learned to think of babies and toddlers in a new, more respectful way. Later, I served as director of Los Angeles Family School in L.A., where another group of very gifted teachers embraced and modeled conflict resolution. I really can't begin to say how much these three experiences have influenced me personally and professionally.

Soon after transitioning from administration to parent education (with Los Angeles Unified School District) I became interested in how conflict resolution works with adults in disputes. I began mediation training with the Dispute Resolution Program, which was affiliated with the Los Angeles City Attorney's Office. I was stunned to learn how similar the conflict-resolution methodology was. Even some of the gnarliest adult disputes looked so much like the ones children have! Not only that, but the very same techniques were deployed in getting to resolution.

In 2007 I opened my own mediation practice, which operates side-by-side with my work in parent education under the banner "I help people talk to each other." My mediation practice has provided me with ample opportunity to work with adults struggling to get along. Layering this experience upon my work in child development, I've arrived at the conclusion that conflict is conflict, and mediation is mediation. I often joke that every dispute in the world boils down to one of two things: 1) You took my stuff; 2) You called me a poopy-head. Or both. It's always about property and/or respect. This is true in the sandbox, the boardroom and, from what I read in the news, at the United Nations as well. Sometimes, after mediation, parties will ask me how I got interested in this line of work. I wish you could see the look on their faces when I tell them I started out as a nursery school teacher!

In my private practice, I am most happy mediating for what I call SWOAPs — people who are Stuck With One Another Permanently. This would be landlords and tenants, neighbors, co-workers, divorced or separated co-parents, and siblings of all ages. (And aren't siblings really the ultimate SWOAPs?)

This book braids together the three dominant strands in my professional life — child development, parent education, and mediation. I hope it addresses conflict resolution for you, the parent or caregiver, in a way that is fresh, thought-provoking, and above all useful.

# SIBLING CONFLICTS, NUISANCE, OR OPPORTUNITY: WHY MEDIATE?

*S*o much has been written about conflict. From mere squabbling to outright war, the subject has captivated researchers and theorists from many disciplines — biology, history, psychology, sociology, neuroscience, and anthropology, to name a handful. What nearly everyone agrees on is that conflict is here to stay. Since that's the case, and since our first conflict partners tend to be siblings, what can we do to make the best of the situation?

I am deeply indebted to Craig E. Runde and Tim A. Flanagan for coining the term "conflict competence." I love this idea! It normalizes conflict and suggests that it's something you could get better at with practice, like knitting or long division or soccer. Although Runde and Flanagan work as facilitators with adults in workplace conflicts, what they have to say has been useful to me in thinking about sibling conflicts as well. After all, siblings are stuck with one another in much the same way co-workers are. As a friend of mine complained: "I didn't choose to be teamed up with Lorraine from Accounting. Our temperaments are quite different. Our work styles aren't compatible. We see the world very differently. She's not someone I would choose for a friend."

Siblings can feel a lot like employees do when they've been

randomly paired up at work. Runde and Flanagan point out that bosses (that would be parents, assuming my metaphor is holding up) are often so uncomfortable with conflict that all disagreements are stifled. This limits creativity and growth; stagnation and resentment can result. By contrast, bosses who view conflict as acceptable and manageable realize that disputes actually offer opportunities for personal development, relationship-building, and deepening of trust. These bosses also understand that, by using sound dispute resolution techniques, they stand a better chance of keeping conflict fair and above-board. Not so with conflicts that are suppressed. As Flanagan and Runde point out, even the best-stifled dispute will somehow manage to surface, and because it hasn't been handled skillfully it will likely explode in personal attacks.

*"I'd like to propose a different approach to the Hopkins account."*

Can become, *"You always have to get your way — you're such a control freak!"* Similarly, at home, *"I just want a turn with the remote."*

Can turn into, *"You're so selfish!"*

Sound familiar? In an environment where conflict is suppressed at all costs, feelings build to the boiling point. And as we've all seen, things can get very, very ugly.

When we mediate for siblings, we accept disputes as naturally occurring. We turn those disputes into an ongoing process through which kids can learn to be conflict-competent. They will take their conflict competence beyond the family circle — to school, to play dates, and to the soccer field. It will accompany them in high school and college, where they will encounter a wider world of unfamiliar people and ideas. Later, they will deploy it at work and in all the nuanced, complex relationships they enter into.

But it takes practice to become conflict-competent. Ruth Beaglehole, founding director of L.A.'s Echo Parenting and Education, captures this so well when she refers to siblinghood as a "workshop for intimacy." This observation shines with Ruth's wisdom and insight. EPE is a community-based organization with an enlightened and respectful approach to child rearing. Ruth and her staff help parents understand that conflicts between siblings are opportunities for kids to learn how to manage conflict in *any* relationship.

Ruth is not alone in her belief that siblinghood — with conflict as part of the package — confers certain advantages. Renown child development expert Lee Salk, author of *What Every Child Would Like His Parents to Know*, agreed. He felt that siblings create stresses for one another and that those stresses, if overcome successfully, provide perspective and adaptability.

Whenever I ask parents of siblings what drives them craziest about their kids' disputes, the answers touch on a number of themes:

- "It's relentless. It feels like it never stops."
- "I feel like they're fighting for control over my ears."
- "They're so mean to each other. They really know how to twist the knife."
- "It's so noisy! It really gets on my nerves."
- "There's so much unfairness."
- "I try so hard not to take sides, but to them it always looks like I'm biased."
- "It's so repetitive. I think I've settled something, and the next day they're at it again."

Mediation addresses all of these issues, but for now let's focus on the parent who thinks she's settled something. What she has probably done is *arbitrate* the conflict. This is the time-honored method parents have used to settle disputes. One or both kids came running to her about a dispute, and she brought them together. She listened to one side of the story, then the other. She then proclaimed her decision. Like a judge handing down a verdict or a referee making a call, she used her authority and wisdom to *arbitrate*. As is usually the case, the decision was win/lose, so one of the kids left happy, the other disgruntled. Not surprisingly, a few days later, the conflict resurfaced.

I think mediation is a better way, and to explain this I need to compare arbitration and mediation more fully.

## What Does Mediation/Arbitration Look Like in the Real World?

In the real world of ADR (Alternative Dispute Resolution, which can be thought of as "staying out of court") arbitration is often a terrific way to resolve a conflict. Basically a scaled-down trial, arbitration is relatively inexpensive and quite efficient. Better still, it puts the decision in the hands of a person, or several persons, who actually know something about the subject matter. A judge may be a brilliant jurist, but he can't run out and get a degree in engineering in order to rule fairly on a construction case. The arbitrator(s) in such a case would likely have a background in contracting, engineering, or architecture.

Medicine is another highly technical field that has embraced arbitration. The preference for having an expert decide, along with the wish to avoid lengthy and expensive legal actions, is why so many medical doctors have an arbitration clause in their agreement to treat. In our lawsuit-happy society, this keeps patients and doctors out of court while allowing malpractice cases to be decided by experts — people with backgrounds in medicine and insurance matters.

One reason that arbitrating these kinds of cases works so well is that the parties are not stuck with one another permanently. If you're angry and dissatisfied enough to take action against your contractor or your doctor, you are not likely to use that person's services again regardless of the outcome of the arbitration. After the conflict, you'll go your separate ways and that will be that. Another reason for arbitration's success is that typically the parties are represented by lawyers. Dispassionate and articulate, the attorneys are expected to maintain a courteous and low-key tone. What the process lacks in emotional depth, it makes up for in civility. However, there are a whole class of people considering legal action who I think do not benefit from arbitration — or from taking their grievance to court, for that matter — precisely because they are in an ongoing relationship. They are:

- Landlords and tenants
- Neighbors
- Family members, such as adult siblings
- Co-workers
- Separating/separated/divorced co-parents

Yes, the SWOAPs. In these disputes, feelings matter, and they matter a lot. More importantly, SWOAPs would still have to interact with one another after a trial or arbitration. Think of it: your neighbor sues you about a conflict over the fence between your properties. One of you leaves the courtroom elated and gloating, and the other is feeling bitter and vengeful. *And you are still neighbors.* The stage is perfectly set for further conflict. Every time you go out to get the mail, the dread of running into that person puts your stomach in knots. In matters such as this one, the win/lose solution is a non-solution. In fact, it may be just one more in a long list of irritants. Resumed conflict is just about inevitable.

Had you mediated with the neighbor, a trained, neutral facilitator (the mediator) would have assisted you in exploring the conflict more deeply. The mediator would have helped you both to discuss the matter respectfully and to search for overlapping interests in order to jointly craft a win/win outcome (or at least what I like to call a "not lose/not lose" one.) The mediator wouldn't give you advice or decide anything. You and the neighbor, not the mediator, would own the outcome. Also, you would have been given the chance to determine how your relationship would look from mediation day forward. (How SWOAPs plan to behave in the aftermath of a dispute is a crucial matter, but it's one that judges and arbitrators rarely address.) All the steps in mediation are necessary in order to turn the corner in a damaged relationship and to make future contact bearable, if not downright comfortable.

Mediation is most urgently needed and most richly rewarding when the parties are SWOAPs. How does this apply to siblings, the ultimate SWOAPs? I think this is a key question, because traditionally arbitration has been the go-to mode used by parents. In dealing with sibling disputes, mediation is more powerful than arbitration in a number of ways.

**Mediation looks for a win/win outcome.** Arbitration is by nature legalistic and fact-finding. It looks to point the finger at a guilty party and reward the wronged party. By contrast, mediation seeks to identify feelings and explore common ground as a means to helping parties attain a joint resolution. Siblings who are used to mediating expect to get something of value from the process. They know that they may not get everything they want, but they will be heard and their needs will be respected. Kids learn from experience that if the parent arbitrates, one person will probably win and the other will lose.

Arbitration activates the "hope versus dread" mindset: *Am I going to be ecstatic or devastated about the outcome?* Naturally, this produces tremendous anxiety. Kids who mediate a lot can feel more relaxed about conflict, so they get accustomed to negotiating in a low-key, businesslike tone. They understand that staying calm soothes their opponent and makes way for good resolutions. They come to expect compromise and to value it above a win/lose outcome.

**Mediation humanizes the conflict partner.** A mediator encourages parties to listen to one another and to re-state what the other person said. This invites respectful dialogue and encourages perspective-taking. It also helps build empathy. Seeing something from another person's viewpoint does not come easily to young children, but learning to do so is fundamental in building healthy relationships. By contrast, in arbitration each party tends to see the conflict partner as "an opponent who might beat me" — a threatening *other* who is just out to thwart him.

**Mediation encourages authenticity.** In arbitration, a lot of intellectual and emotional energy gets squandered in the effort to persuade the arbitrator. The focus is on the deciding party (the arbitrator) instead of the conflict partner; what should be a conversation turns into a campaign for that single all-important vote. No wonder parents feel like the rope in a tug-of-war!

Mediation keeps kids' hearts and minds focused on one another in order to arrive at a jointly crafted resolution. A child who feels calm and focused on a win/win outcome is likelier to be honest about what happened as well as her feelings about what happened. By contrast, the child who is anxious about being beaten in a competition operates more strategically and may be tempted to tweak the facts in her favor and to act more aggrieved than she is really feeling. These distortions and exaggerations can be unconscious. It's hard for people to behave well in high-stakes, emotionally charged contests. As we've all seen, cheating and over-dramatizing often accompany a tensely competitive situation. When we arbitrate a lot, we may be unintentionally inviting kids to bend the truth and "carry on" just the way the people in courtroom reality shows do! After several repetitions, untruthfulness about facts and feelings becomes ritualized and ingrained. Neurologically, it actually becomes a sort of memory. Like all of us, children can get very attached to inauthentic stories, emotions, and roles.

**Mediation looks for overlapping interests.** Arbitration tends to highlight differences, so it can be polarizing. The very process of pinpointing differences can heighten conflict, leaving the parties even angrier at one another than when they started out. Mediation seeks to look a little deeper. One way to do this is to try to separate *positions* from *interests*. In negotiation terms, a *position* is what the person says he has to have. An *interest* is why he believes he needs it. When the mediator asks the kids why they want what they want, she is helping them explore overlapping interests, which can result in a softening of their positions. This advances the process to the problem-solving stage.

**Mediation repositions the kids to feel "it's you and me against the problem."** One of the key steps in mediation is brainstorming solutions. Mediation is essentially a collaborative process. This is not true of arbitration. Brainstorming solutions is an activity that pits the two children, working as a team, against a shared challenge. This presents a useful and significant shift from the initial "you and me against each other" posture. Mediation engages cooperativeness and reduces competition.

**Mediation allows the parent to facilitate neutrally, without judging or refereeing.** Arbitration positions the parent to hand down a verdict or make a call. Because parents desire fairness, this can be very stressful. It's frustrating too, because fairness can feel like a moving target. If you handed down decisions in favor of Jeffrey three times last week, you may feel uncomfortable deciding (yet again!) against his brother today. Add to that the likelihood that, whatever you decide, you are sure to hear the familiar wail, "That's not faaaiiirrrrrr!"

**Mediation has the power to put certain conflicts to rest.** This is because it addresses underlying issues rather than just superficial complaints. An arbitrated decision, being win/lose, usually produces a gloater and a vengeance-seeker. It's not hard to see how this can be a perfect setup for continued conflict. Mediation, by getting to the heart of the matter, does a better job of interrupting a negative cycle — those recurring arguments that can be so maddening. We often see siblings fighting in a style that could be called "theme and variation." An argument keeps resurfacing, slightly altered, but with mostly familiar elements. It's like another verse to the same song, with the arbitration acting as chorus. The parent listens to both kids, hands down a decision (arbitrates, in other words) and sure enough, a couple of days or weeks later, here it comes again! What has happened is this: the arbitrator has shut off a distress signal without examining the underlying source of distress. The signal re-sets itself through the invention of another variation on the same argument. Arbitration merely sets the stage for endless re-enactments of the dispute. A mediated solution, though more time-consuming in the short term, delves a little deeper and gets at some of the feelings lying underneath the conflict. This offers a greater chance of putting the matter to rest.

**Mediation teaches children to be conflict-competent and conflict-independent.** When you mediate, you are providing your kids with a structure for examining conflict as well as language for expressing feelings, wants, and needs. In this way, they learn to negotiate with one another while gradually weaning themselves from needing your support when disagreements arise. One of the best definitions of parenthood I ever heard was, "It's your job to do yourself out of a job." Seen in this light, mediation is very empowering. If you consistently arbitrate your children's disputes, they will have no option but to return again and again in search of expertise and authority. In truth, each child *is* the expert concerning his own feelings and wants, and the process of mediating guides him toward self-mastery and a sense of personal authority.

**Mediation deals with more than the tip of the iceberg**. Arbitration tends to stick with what is visible and obvious, not delving or probing to discover what underlies the conflict. A seemingly petty dispute can be masking a deeper problem. Often the disputants themselves have no idea what's going on below the surface. But the safety of emotional honesty calms both parties. Once they can relax and exchange information with each other about how they are feeling, interesting new information often surfaces. This leads to self-awareness and empathy — which in turn makes way for problem-solving.

**Mediation is likelier to produce compliance than an arbitrated decision.** It's only human nature — if there is buy-in from the parties themselves, they tend to be more cooperative with the resolution. After all, the contract is theirs; they created it together. This is demonstrably true. According to California Association of Mediation Professionals (CAMP), an organization that provides volunteer mediators to courts in the Los Angeles area, "Statistics around the country have shown that only approximately 25 percent of [Small Claims Court] plaintiffs collect any money on their judgments, and often those collecting any money are not able to collect the entire amount. However, if you sit down with the other side and work out an agreement that both of you are comfortable with, your chances of actually receiving that money increase dramatically. We rarely receive a call from a party complaining that the agreement reached is not being complied with." It's the same with kids. When they own the resolution, they take greater responsibility for its enactment.

**Mediation accepts, channels, and defuses strong emotions.** Arbitration, being more legalistic in nature, looks for *just the facts*. However, in avoiding any examination of deep emotions, an arbitration process often leaves the parties feeling emotionally raw and not finished with key elements of the dispute. As every parent knows, teeny-tiny people do not have teeny-tiny emotions. Quite the contrary — they experience their emotions in huge capital letters! At these times, you can't reason with them, and you can't distract them. Add to all of this the fact that the young child has poor self-control, a short attention span and a limited vocabulary for expressing all these varied and intense feelings. Mediation offers a structure in which children can compose themselves, stay focused, and express what they're feeling.

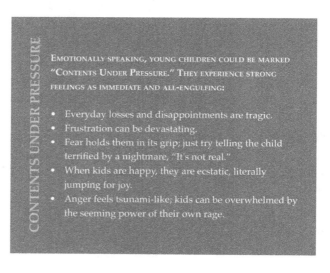

EMOTIONALLY SPEAKING, YOUNG CHILDREN COULD BE MARKED "CONTENTS UNDER PRESSURE." THEY EXPERIENCE STRONG FEELINGS AS IMMEDIATE AND ALL-ENGULFING:

- Everyday losses and disappointments are tragic.
- Frustration can be devastating.
- Fear holds them in its grip; just try telling the child terrified by a nightmare, "It's not real."
- When kids are happy, they are ecstatic, literally jumping for joy.
- Anger feels tsunami-like; kids can be overwhelmed by the seeming power of their own rage.

CONTENTS UNDER PRESSURE

**Mediation helps forceful personalities learn to compromise and teaches meeker types to stand their ground.** We're born with different types of personalities, and temperament profoundly influences how we deal with disputes. The prospect of conflict presents a fight or flight response in just about everyone. It isn't hard to figure out who is inclined to fight and who tends to flee. The purpose of mediation isn't to change lions into lambs or vice versa. However, if a naturally bold and aggressive child doesn't learn something about negotiation and compromise, he could be seen as overbearing right into adulthood. Likewise, if a reticent, mild-mannered child doesn't learn to stick up for his needs and wants, he might be a pushover others take advantage of. Mediation helps nudge these extreme personalities (we can think of them as having "liabilities of temperament") a little toward center, providing solid, real-life coping skills in the process.

| MEDIATION VS. ARBITRATION | | |
|---|---|
| **MEDIATION** | **ARBITRATION** |
| Emphasizes feelings and common ground | Seeks facts; is legalistic in approach |
| Looks for a win-win outcome | Results in a win/lose outcome |
| Seeks to be low-key and businesslike | Produces "high-stakes" anxiety |
| Calms the parties | Agitates the parties |
| Humanizes the conflict partner | Demonizes the conflict partner |
| Fosters respect, empathy, perspective | Reinforces self-centeredness |
| Emphasizes authenticity | Emphasizes strategizing |
| Fosters honesty about the facts | Tempts children to distort the truth |
| Encourages honesty about feelings | Invites over-acting and "drama" |
| Seeks to identify overlapping interests | Tends to polarize conflict partners |
| Separates position from interest | Buttresses opposing positions |
| Reframes conflict as "us against the problem" | Reinforces "us against each other" |
| Stresses collaboration | Stresses competition |
| Frees parent to facilitate from a neutral position | Forces parent to judge/decide/advise |
| Reduces the need for a re-match | Sets stage for continued conflict |
| Can put a conflict to rest | Promotes ongoing conflict via postponement |
| Fosters independence in resolving disputes | Perpetuates dependence on "judge/referee" |
| Promotes emotional mastery, self-regulation | Ignores/sidesteps/blocks strong emotion |
| Looks beneath the surface | Focuses on the "tip of the iceberg" |
| Prompts disputants to comply with resolution | Produces resistance and non-compliance |
| Teaches compromise/standing one's ground | Fails to address "liabilities of temperament" |

We all seek a more harmonious, peaceful family life. In what follows, I invite you to think about peace not as a state of being (the absence of conflict) but rather as a process (a way of handling conflict.)

## 2

# WHAT DOES MEDIATION LOOK LIKE?

*T*here is a time-honored format (protocol) for mediation. With slight variations, it's what most mediators do when they sit down with parties to resolve a conflict. I wish I could say I invented it, but I didn't. What I did do is create the acronym TABMOC (*combat* spelled backward) to help you stay on track while reminding you that mediation really is the opposite of fighting.

Before beginning, invite the kids to mediate. If you are new to this, some explanation is necessary. Tailor what you say to the kids' maturity level and attention span. Reassure them that you are going to try to ask good questions, but you are not going to give advice or tell them how to solve the problem; you want it to be their solution. It's also important to stress that you are not going to take sides. You will also want to establish ground rules. Begin by offering a few of your own (respectful dialogue, taking turns listening and talking, telling the truth — whatever matters to you.) In my own mediation practice, I ask my clients to "Keep it REAL."

**KEEP IT REAL**

**RESPECT**
Use a conversational tone of voice.

Refrain from using insulting body language (e.g., rolling eyes, turning away).

No name-calling, put-downs, insults, or sarcasm. Take turns, avoid interrupting.

**EFFORT**
Have an open mind and an open heart.

Recognize that there is no "microwave" solution to a complex issue.

**AUTHENTICITY**
Be as honest as you know how to be about the facts.

Be as honest as you know how to be about your feelings and reactions.

**LISTENING**
Listen more than you talk.

Listen to understand rather than merely to rebut or refute. (Remember that understanding does not necessarily equal agreement.)

Once, I was getting ready to mediate between two parent couples in a school setting. Several administrators were in attendance. There were a lot of people in the room and tensions were high. I presented my ground rules and one of the parties blurted out, "Wow, if everybody behaved like this all the time, you'd be out of work!" This got us all laughing, and the mediation was off to a good start.

It's usually not hard to get people to agree to ground rules.

Setting standards makes people feel safe. Maybe this is because each party figures it's the other person, not himself, who is likely to "lose it." After getting buy-in on your ground rules, ask your kids if they have any others that they would like to suggest as well. Before beginning, make sure everyone agrees to the rules that have been put on the table. Not only does this help set the tone; the commitment stands as something you can refer back to if anyone's behavior goes out of bounds, which I guarantee will happen from time to time. Perhaps your family will invent and agree upon a set of ground rules that you can put up on the fridge or family bulletin board.

Over time, your introduction will become streamlined. However, I urge you never to slight or skip this step. Recapping your role, your neutrality, and the ground rules sets an intention for all of you. It will get things off on the right foot and help steady the process. Now you're ready to begin mediating, using the the TABMOC protocol.

### T Is for Talking

Invite each child to talk about the situation. Give everyone plenty of time to say what is on his or her mind. Get them to talk about what happened *and how they felt about it*. In this way, you help them frame I-messages: "I feel [emotion] when you [verb]." You may have to use active listening techniques — "It sounds like you got pretty discouraged when you heard that." — to nudge them toward getting at the emotional content. (More about I-messages and active listening in Chapter Nine.)

### A Is for Acknowledging

Although you will be summarizing and validating as you go, be sure to encourage each child to say what is on the other child's mind by re-stating it, even if this feels repetitive. Be sure the listener's reiteration includes the emotional piece of the speaker's message. (Often the second speaker will try to use the Acknowledge phase to launch a rebuttal against what she just heard. Remind her that this is just the "talk and listen" part of the mediation and that her turn to speak and be heard is coming up next.)

Letting each child speak and be heard is critically important because it helps both children "feel felt," in the words of Daniel Siegel and Mary Hartzell (see *Parenting from the Inside Out* in the Annotated Bibliography at the end of this book.) When we hear our opponent accurately reflect what is bothering us — *and why* — we calm down. Feeling soothed prepares us to get down to the business of problem-solving. Not only does Acknowledgment oil the wheels of the mediation at hand; it reinforces a useful habit for responding to distressed people in general. In this way, every mediation serves as a rehearsal for reacting effectively in any emotionally charged situation.

---

Sometimes it's best to use a TA-TA process (Party #1 Talks, Party #2 Acknowledges, then Party #2 Talks, Party #1 Acknowledges.) Other times, TT-AA works better (both parties Talk, then both parties Acknowledge.) This is always a judgment call, and it can depend on how the mediation is flowing. If a child is immature or very emotionally overwrought, it's going to be challenging to restate what is bothering his sibling before he, too, has had his say. In this case, TT-AA might be the preferred format. Just be sure that both children get a chance to be heard and to demonstrate that they have heard.

---

### B Is for Brainstorming

Invite the kids to come up with solutions. No idea is too crazy or far-fetched. Don't be surprised if "kid solutions" sound a lot different from what you feel is reasonable or fair. If the ideas are flying fast and furious, you may want to write them down. If no one can think of anything, an outrageous or silly suggestion from you might jog them: "Shall we write to Santa Claus, and see what he thinks?"

Once you have more than two suggestions on the table, things can get very interesting. I think of it as The Magic of Idea #3. The first two suggestions are usually along the lines of "I get to have it" / "No, I get to have it." Once this falls flat, the kids realize they have to get more creative. A third idea means that someone has detached from his position enough to imagine a fresh option. The very act of doing this may help the other party to loosen her grip on her position. Here you may detect a significant shift — when "you and me against each other" becomes "you and me against the problem."

Brainstorming is a good time to try for balance. (It may not be enough for Lisa to say she will stop calling Quentin a baby when he annoys her. Is there a specific annoying behavior that Quentin can agree to stop? A desired behavior that he can try to adopt? That's the essence of win/win.)

Brainstorming is creative and collaborative. Try to keep the kids from critiquing or comparing the various ideas as they are offered. Ridicule and criticism shut down creativity like nothing else, and Brainstorming should be an unfettered, freewheeling part of the mediation process.

You may have to stifle your own critical thoughts too. The resolution they are striving for is theirs (more about your neutrality in Chapter Six and more about fairness below, under "Organization.") Once all the suggestions have been offered, you are ready to move on from Brainstorming.

### M Is for Mulling-Over

This is the time to compare all the ideas and to begin negotiating about them. If kids have objections, they should be encouraged to state respectfully what they don't like about someone else's suggestion, or how they would tweak it to make it more acceptable. Here you can sometimes help if you notice that Party #1 wants such-and-such but still hasn't put anything on the table as a concession. You can gently probe to see if Party #2 needs or wants something in return. Often an idea that sounded terrible five minutes ago starts to sound pretty good if it's accompanied by something of value in exchange. A lot of hybridizing happens during negotiations, especially in cases where there are a lot of options on the table. Kids are very nimble thinkers. They may take the front end of one idea and hook it on to the back end of another. Once that happens, they may really have something!

### O Is for Organizing

You may have been doing some organizing already, writing some things down and putting side issues that have popped up in the "Parking Lot" for later. (More about the Parking Lot in Chapter Six.) Here's where you try to pull everything together in order to prepare some kind of contract.

It's the time to ask lots of clarifying questions and hash out the terms and the wording that everyone can live with. It's also the time to get specific. Think journalism: who, what, when, where, and how. This is not the time for glib or vague promises. To the extent possible, goof-proof the agreement by nailing down the details. Is it realistic? Is it durable? If a big brother agrees to be nicer, what will that look like? The little sister might be envisioning an invitation to eat lunch with her brother's group at school, whereas he's thinking more in terms of simply agreeing not to make faces at her during dinner. In other words, try to align promises with expectations. If one child has agreed to something that you worry is unfair to him, you could build into the contract that everyone meet again in a week to review how things are going. (There is nothing quite like giving in or giving up and then having to live with the consequences for a bit. It will make anyone a more careful negotiator going forward.) It's also a good idea to build in protocols for any lapses that might occur. ("What will happen if Marissa forgets to make her bed?") Help the parties think through what they will have to do to change their behavior according to the contract. ("What will it take for you to do this differently?") Neuroscientists tell us that a mental rehearsal can prepare us to follow through later, by harnessing mindfulness and self-control.

. . .

### C Is for Contracting

Each child should commit to the terms of the agreement. Usually, a sincere verbal contract should do it, but signing a clear and precise written contract adds solemnity to the occasion. Or, each child could write a short letter to the other detailing what each is promising to do (or not do) and give it to the sibling. Putting it in their own writing provides the kids with another kind of mental walk-through. This could help an impulsive child to curb his behavior. In closing, thank the kids for their time and effort, their honesty — whatever seems appropriate to you.

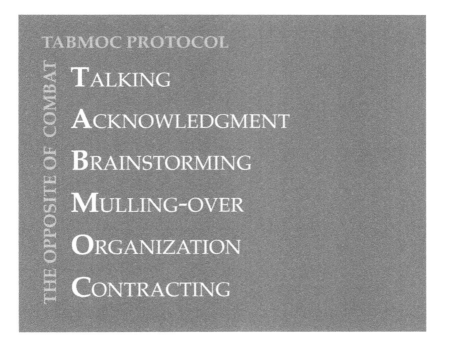

TABMOC PROTOCOL

THE OPPOSITE OF COMBAT

**T**ALKING

**A**CKNOWLEDGMENT

**B**RAINSTORMING

**M**ULLING-OVER

**O**RGANIZATION

**C**ONTRACTING

Every mediation looks different. In comparing these steps to the various scenarios in Chapter Three, you will see that they all follow the same general arc. However, a step requiring a great deal of attention in one mediation may get glossed over in another. A lot depends on the ages and maturity of the disputants, the complexity of the dispute, and the level of familiarity these particular children have with mediation.

# 3

# TABMOC IN ACTION

## Sample Mediation Scenarios

he scenarios in this chapter should give you an idea of what mediation looks like. As you'll see, mediations all have the same basic structure, yet no two are the same. (Note: In an attempt to make these scenarios a little easier to follow, I have named all the siblings alphabetically by birth order.)

# MEDIATION SCENARIO 1

## "It's Not About the Money"

Jesse and Eli are five-and-a half-year-old identical twins who have no other brothers or sisters. This has been a challenging year for them. Having gone to a small, intimate preschool where they were in the same classroom, they enrolled five months ago in a large elementary school with two kindergartens. Whereas before they had always been invited together on play dates and to birthday parties, the game plan has changed somewhat now that each has a classroom of his own. Jesse had always been more independent and outgoing than Eli, so it's no surprise that he has had less trouble navigating the challenges of this new social situation. In fact, he's had three or four play dates; Eli has been invited on only one so far.

Now, the inevitable has happened. This is something the boys' parents, Marlene and George, have been somewhat dreading. One of Jesse's new friends, Sean, has invited him for a sleepover. The big day is here; it's Saturday morning. Even though he's not due at Sean's house for hours, Jesse is excitedly packing for the big trip — you would think he was going on an expedition into the outback! In between chores, Marlene is coming in and out of the boys' room, offering packing suggestions to Jesse as well as making edits. She notices that Eli has been hanging around, not saying anything but observing the process intently. Suddenly, Jesse pops behind his bed and reappears clutching a tattered box of Chutes and Ladders®. Just as he plunks it on top of the mountain of supplies sitting in his open suitcase, Eli explodes in angry tears.

> Eli: You can't take C&L! It's not fair! (He grabs it out of the suitcase and tries to run out of the room. Jesse tackles him and grabs the box back, but not before its contents spill everywhere. Now both boys are in tears and shouting angrily. Marlene hears the commotion and hurries in.)
>
> Marlene: Boys, boys! Wow, you are both *really* upset. Let's sit down and talk.
>
> Jesse: I don't want to talk! I want him to pick up all the C&L pieces and leave me alone so I can pack!
>
> Eli: He started it! He grabbed the box from me, and it spilled. What a baby!
>
> Marlene: Jesse, you do need to pack, that's right. But luckily we still have a few hours. And Eli, you sound like you have a lot to talk about. Come over and sit down, both of you. (She steers them to a place where they can all sit comfortably on the floor.)
>
> We're going to talk, and we're going to listen. I want you to use your regular voices and not insult each other while we do this. I'm not going to decide anything; this is your discussion. Can you agree to that? (Both boys grumpily agree.) OK, who wants to go first? (Eli is glowering, just barely keeping his emotions in check.)
>
> Jesse: I was packing my stuff, and I was putting C&L in my suitcase. All of a sudden Eli was grabbing it and yelling at me.

Marlene: How did that make you feel?

Jesse: I dunno ... mad?

Marlene: It sounds like maybe you were a little surprised too ...

Jesse: I was *really* surprised.

Marlene: So you were really surprised, and then you were mad. Eli, what about you? Tell me what happened ...

Eli: (Slowly) I was watching him pack, and then I saw him put C&L in the suitcase. (Getting excited) It's not *fair* for him to take C&L on the sleepover!

Marlene: So that feels really unfair to you.

Eli: Yes! It's not fair!

Marlene: Eli, can you tell us what Jesse said happened?

Eli: (Long pause) Jesse said he was packing C&L, and I grabbed it out of the suitcase, and it surprised him.

Marlene: (Gently) It surprised him and made him *mad*.

Eli (Still very grumpy): ... surprised him and made him *mad* ...

Marlene: Jesse, can you tell what was happening for Eli?

Jesse: He chased me and grabbed the box. (Getting louder, indignantly) It made a huge mess!

Marlene: I mean before that. What did he see, and what did he feel? Do you remember what he said to us about that?

Jesse: He said he saw me put the box in the suitcase ... and he thought it wasn't fair. That's so dumb!

Marlene: I think you're forgetting one of the rules we agreed on. No insulting language?

Jesse: OK.

Marlene: So Eli felt it was unfair. (Now she is stumped. Surely she's missing something! There is a very long silence — a full minute perhaps. She is hoping someone will enlighten her as to why this game is suddenly such a big deal, but no one says anything.)

You know what I'm wondering? I'm wondering why suddenly today, at this very moment, C&L matters so much to both of you. I'm curious to know why. (Another very long pause.) Neither of you has played with it for over a year. And right now it's very, very special and important. (Both boys fidget for a long while; no one makes eye contact.)

Eli: Mom, *you* know.

Marlene: I really don't, Eli. Please help me understand. What's so important about C&L?

Eli: Remember Together Time? Grandma said when we turned three we could finally play nice together, so she gave us this game to share? And we used to play it all the time? (Turning to Jesse) And we would have graham crackers with cream cheese, and we would drink apple juice ...

Jesse: (Quietly) I remember ...

Marlene: Wow, Eli — it sounds like you have really special,

really happy memories of playing C&L with Jesse. And Jesse, you remember that too.

Eli (Starting to cry again, no longer angrily but very sadly) That's why it isn't fair!

Marlene: (After a long pause so Jesse can take in Eli's reaction.) Eli, I can see that this makes you really sad. I wonder if it felt unfair to you because maybe you want the game to be just for you and Jesse. (She sneaks a look at Jesse, who is now wearing a more interested, sympathetic expression. After a very long pause, she takes the plunge.) Jesse, do you feel like it would be the same playing C&L with Sean as it would with Eli?

Jesse: Not really ...

Marlene: Talk to Eli a little about that.

Jesse: It's different. It will be fun to play with Sean, but you're my *brother*. It's different.

Marlene: It sounds like maybe it's *special* when you play with your brother.

Jesse: Yeah.

Marlene: All those memories make it more of a big deal.

Jesse: Uh-huh.

Marlene: (Slowly, choosing her words carefully) Being brothers *is* a really big deal. It's a really special connection you two have with each other. It sounds like when you play C&L, you're kind of *celebrating* that connection. (Waits for this to this sink in.) Does anyone want to say anything?

Eli: I'm kinda sad we don't play C&L anymore.

Marlene: Eli, do you wish you could play C&L with Jesse sometime soon? (Eli, still snuffling, nods very emphatically.) Would you like to ask him?

Eli: (Turning to his brother) Can we?

Jesse: Sure.

Marlene: Do you want to plan a time? (They are stuck.) How about tomorrow afternoon after we bring Jesse and the game home? (The boys nod their agreement.) OK, I'll be sure to lay in some grammies and cream cheese and apple juice! And now we have some C&L to clean up ...

## "It's Not About the Money" Mediation Deconstructed

Sometimes kids' disputes seem to come out of left field, and this one really took Marlene by surprise. But she kept her cool and remained very neutral. She let both boys talk, and then made sure that each could (with some necessary prompting) describe the other brother's position and emotional response. Because of their age and the level of feeling they were having, she used T-T-A-A instead of T-A-T-A. In other words, they both had a chance to talk and vent before having to acknowledge what the other was feeling. Once they both felt heard, they calmed down. That freed things up for an exploration of what was really going on.

It seems Marlene was open to the possibility that there might be a big fat iceberg under that tip. Maybe it wasn't really about C&L at all. Mediators often say, "It's not about the money." Every mediator has seen the stakes of a conflict — the money, the demands, the hurt — evaporate in the face of an apology or some other meaningful gesture.

Marlene was wise to allow for silence. Sometimes the parties will fill the quiet. At the very least, it gave her time to ask herself, "What on earth is going on here?" Not feeling pressured to be The Wise One or The Expert, Marlene simply stated her bewilderment to the boys, saying, in effect, "Help me out here." She might have been tempted to say, "Oh for goodness' sake, Eli, you haven't looked at that game in over a year, don't be such a poor sport!" or "Look, Jesse, you've got a play date and he doesn't — just be nice, and leave the darn game home!" By leaving a big wide space for the boys to fill, she allowed *them* to get to the heart of the issue. It wasn't really about the game after all. Eli's "iceberg" turned out to be quite a sensitive matter — his forlorn worry that the brother who had always been his social anchor might forsake him.

After Eli's passionate outburst about Together Time, Marlene knew that he needed some very specific reassurances. She realized that, even though she could say a lot of eloquent, touchy-feely things about the twins' relationship, Eli needed some of that to come directly from Jesse. She also knew that Jesse would require a lot of help telling Eli how cherished he was. Trusting Jesse to come up with something positive and kind, she asked, " ... do you feel like it would be the same playing C&L with Sean as it would with Eli?" Then, without moralizing or imposing a lot of "shoulds" about how brothers act toward one another, Marlene provided needed content to this part of the talk by expanding on Jesse's response. All he said was, "It's different. It will be fun to play with Sean, but you're my *brother*. It's different." Marlene offered this interpretation: "... being brothers is a really big deal ... it's a really special connection you two have with each other ... when you play C&L, you're kind of *celebrating* that connection ... " These are ideas a five-year-old child can't be expected to express, even if he feels them wholeheartedly. By helping her less-expressive child match his brother's emotional level, Marlene was doing what mediators call Power Balancing, which we'll look at in greater detail in Chapter Six.

Marlene brought things to a successful close by making sure that a satisfying reunion match got scheduled. She even put in a light remark about the game returning home with Jesse. In doing so, she was actually goof-proofing and checking in. This would have been an opportunity for Eli to re-state his objection to the game being taken on the overnight. If he had still been adamant, the rest of the mediation would have centered on negotiating about that. However, as Marlene sensed, Eli had let go of his position. This is because that position had only been fronting for a deeper and more troubling concern. Once he had aired his hurt and gotten the reassurances he needed about the uniqueness and durability of his relationship with Jesse, Eli no longer felt invested in fighting over a board game.

During the mediation, Marlene was able to put aside her personal reaction ("It's so silly to fight over something they haven't looked at in months.") She was also able to refrain from setting an agenda or outcome. She allowed the boys freedom to explore without restrictions, other than providing and maintaining ground rules. When she got stuck, she shared this with them. She looked for feelings under feelings; as it turned out, Jesse was surprised *before* he got angry, and Eli's sadness and worry were hiding just below the surface of his indignation. She deployed her intuition, as when she made the big leap of faith and asked Jesse point-blank if playing C&L with Sean would be the same as playing it with his brother. Ultimately, the boys owned the resolution. What Marlene got was the discovery of Eli's interior struggle, the satisfaction of allowing Jesse to reassure him, and the opportunity to help the twins "celebrate" (her word) their special bond.

# MEDIATION SCENARIO 2

## "A Room of One's Own"

Sasha (13) and Sylvia (10) have shared a room since Sylvia was three months old. The girls have had all the usual squabbles common to siblings who share living space. To make matters worse, Sylvia is the messy, pack rat type whereas her sister is something of a neatnik. Once, when they were five and eight, their despairing father tried to subdue a conflict by putting masking tape on the floor between their beds to delineate the two halves of the room. Later that afternoon, this backfired horribly when Sasha refused to give Sylvia permission to cross her zone in order to get to the bathroom, and Sylvia wet her pants. Needless to say, the masking tape was removed, and Sasha had a good talking-to. Dad's blunder has acquired a place of honor in the family legend, and today everyone — even Sylvia — laughs about it. But it stands as a reminder that things can get ugly, and that arbitrated solutions, especially hasty ones that haven't been goof-proofed, can fail miserably.

Starting around the time Sasha began middle school last year, she has become moodier. Once a pretty good sport about including Sylvia in her activities, she's now dismissive, rolling her eyes at things her younger sister says. When she has friends over, they often exclude Sylvia, who in turn pesters them to involve her. This evening after dinner, the girls are in their room. Sasha, having finished her homework, is texting a friend about a boy they both think is cute. Sylvia, who only just now excavated her workbook from amidst the debris on her desk, is trying to get started on her homework. Suddenly, their parents hear loud screams coming from the girls' room. "Your turn to mediate," their mom nudges their dad, Jeff. "Wish me luck," he says, heaving himself from the couch with a sigh.

Jeff: (Knocks and enters the girls' room) What's going on? (Sasha is on her bed, cell phone in hand. Sylvia is standing over her, fists on hips, looking furious.)

Sylvia: I'm trying to get my homework done and all Sasha does is giggle and shriek with that stupid Eva! I can't concentrate or get my work done!

Sasha: It's not my fault you're such a procrastinator! My homework is finished and I'm just relaxing and having a little fun with my friend.

Sylvia: You're making so much noise I can't do my work!

Jeff: (Settling on the foot of the bed and patting a spot for Sylvia to join them) OK, OK, I think we need to have a chat (his word for mediation.) Do you remember the ground rules?

Sasha: (Glaring at Sylvia) No yelling!

Sylvia: No name-calling! (This sounds like an accusation.)

Jeff: Right. And I'd like you both to speak respectfully and work hard on solving the problem together. Are we agreed? (Sasha rolls her eyes and Sylvia huffs, but neither girl voices an objection. Jeff decides to take this as a yes.) Who wants to go first?

Sylvia: (Taking it down a notch or two) Well, I just found my homework and started on it. Sasha got a text from Eva …

Jeff: Who's Eva?

Sasha: My new friend at school. She just moved here from Newcastle …

Sylvia: And she's making so much noise I can't get my work done! They keep giggling about some stupid — some boy. Sasha didn't used to act so weird.

Jeff: Sasha, what's bothering Sylvia?

Sasha: I'm already finished with my homework, and she doesn't want me to be having any fun.

Jeff: (Suppressing a smile) Well, there may be some truth in that, but what I meant to ask is, what did Sylvia *tell* us is bothering her?

Sasha: She said she's trying to do her homework, and my giggling is bothering her.

Jeff: And?

Sasha: Something about "I didn't used to act so weird." (Indignantly) What is that supposed to mean?

Jeff: Would you like to ask her?

Sasha: (Turning to Sylvia) What's up with that?

Sylvia: (Slowly, feeling a little on the spot) Well … we used to talk about horses … and movies … and princesses and stuff and now it's boys, boys, boys …

Jeff: It's hard to understand how things are changing for Sasha now that she's a teenager.

Sylvia: I guess ...

Jeff: Your turn, Sasha. What's bothering you about this situation?

Sasha: OK, so I finish my homework, I just want to text with my friend, and here's Sylvia complaining and making remarks about Eva.

Sylvia: We don't even know this person Eva! (Jeff is caught by surprise. Sylvia sounds so *parental*!)

Jeff: We can get back to that in a minute. For now, I'm going to put Eva in the Parking Lot. (He fumbles for a paper and pencil and writes this down.) Sylvia, can you say what Sasha said?

Sylvia: She finished her homework, and she wanted to fool around with Eva and text and stuff.

Jeff: And?

Sylvia: And I guess I was saying mean stuff about their texting and the laughing. (Turning to Sasha) I'm sorry. (Jeff glances over at Sasha, who shows no reaction.)

Jeff: (Gently) I think I just heard an apology.

Sasha (Offhand, but making brief eye contact with Sylvia) S'okay ... I guess ... (very long pause) ... thanks.

Jeff: So what I'm hearing is your schedules are sort of ... not in sync ... and that, Sasha, things are changing for you, which is confusing to Sylvia ... (He trails off, wondering *where in the world is this thing headed?*)

Sasha: (With heat) I just wish I had some privacy! (Jeff shoots a quick look at Sylvia and sees that she is hurt by this, but he doesn't quite know what to do with it.)

Sylvia: Well it's my room too. And my desk is here and all my books and my papers ...

Jeff: I wonder how Sasha could get some privacy for her phone calls and texting and teenage stuff ...

Sasha: Where am I supposed to go? The laundry room?

Jeff: (Blandly) Well, that's one idea. Let's think of some others.

Sylvia: How about the family room?

Sasha: What if someone's watching TV? What if I want *privacy*? (There is an uncomfortable silence. Jeff is not sure why, but he scribbles the word "privacy" on the paper.)

Sylvia: What about the back porch? It's kind of like a room. It's got four walls and a roof and no one ever goes back there.

Sasha: (With indignation) Penelope goes there! That's where her *cat box* is!

Jeff: (Feeling the heat — and sarcasm — rising) Does the cat box have to be there? Is it possible that the back porch could be fixed up so it would be suitable for you?

Sylvia: (Thinking fast) We could move the cat box to ... um ... to the alcove off the kitchen ... maybe I could help you fix up the porch! (A very long pause. This is a tough sell. She brightens.) You could take some of our posters from the room ...

Jeff: There's space in there for the big easy chair we have stored in the garage ...

Sylvia: (Pointing) You could have that little table for your cell phone and charger.

Sasha: I'm not sure I would like it ...

Jeff: 'Course not, I'm not sure either. No one knows how it will be. You want to do this for a trial period? If it doesn't work out for you we can meet again and come up with a different solution ... (Both girls nod yes, Sylvia quickly and Sasha after a pause. He turns to Sasha.) How long do you think is fair?

Sasha: Um ... I guess three or four weeks.

Jeff: Can we round that off to a month? (She nods. He glances at the Parking Lot.) So, Sylvia, back to your question about Eva. Do you want to just come out and ask Sasha about her?

Sylvia: Yes! Who is she? Why can't I meet her?

Jeff: Whoa, Sylvia, let's not assume anything. You say, "why can't I meet her?" as if there's some big rule that you can't. Can you try to ask the question another way?

Sylvia: (Somewhat shyly, to Sasha) Can I meet her?

Sasha: Sure ... I guess.

Jeff: What would that look like?

Sylvia: (Pause ... light bulb!) You could invite her for pizza and a movie with us this Sunday night!

Sasha: Um ... OK.

Jeff: Great idea! I'll check with Mom to see if that fits her schedule too. I better start writing this stuff down. (He begins writing and notices the word "privacy.") I look forward to meeting Eva too! (Long pause.) Um, something that came up earlier is still rattling in my brain. Let's see if I can recapture it. Sylvia, when Sasha said earlier that she wanted privacy, you looked so sad. How did it feel to hear that?

Sylvia: Bad ...

Jeff: Talk a little about that.

Sylvia: I guess ... we used to do stuff together and everything has changed. I feel ... (she's stuck.)

Jeff: A little left behind?

Sasha: (Hotly) Am I supposed to feel *guilty* because I'm a *teenager*?

Jeff: Not at all. I'm just trying to understand what's going on here. Sasha, as your dad, I want to understand that you're maturing and needing more time alone. And Sylvia, as your dad, I respect your feeling of loss.

Sylvia: Loss?! (She looks stricken.)

Jeff: Um ... *temporary* loss. I hope this doesn't sound preachy or corny ... but I'm remembering when your Uncle Robert stopped shooting hoops with me and started driving and dating girls and spending more time away from the house ...

with guys his age. I felt like the bus had left without me! I wanted my parents to *make* him do stuff with me but they wouldn't. It was hard. Then a couple of years later I sort of caught up with him, and we started hanging out together again. The summer before he left for college was really memorable ... for both of us, I think. (Long pause while the girls take this in.)

Sasha: It's not like Sylvia and I can't still do *some* stuff together. (Thinking hard) Um ... I was planning to walk to the mall Sunday to spend the gift certificate Bubbie sent me for Chanukah. (Turning to her sister) Do you want to bring yours along and shop with me?

Sylvia: (Clearly thrilled) Yes!

Jeff: Cool! (The girls exchange glances. Dad is so *un*cool. Now he's scribbling some more.) So, we have four agreements.

- First, Sylvia is going to help us fix up the back porch as a getaway for Sasha.
- Second, Sasha is going to take phone calls and noisy text exchanges in her getaway, so she can have privacy and so Sylvia can do her homework in peace. It will be a month-long trial.
- Third, we're going to invite Eva over so Sylvia can meet her. So we can all meet her!
- Number four, you are planning to go together to the mall Sunday.

Did I get everything? (The girls give their assent and Jeff gets up to leave.) Thanks — film at eleven!

## "A ROOM OF ONE'S OWN" MEDIATION DECONSTRUCTED

An arbitrated decision in this case might have looked quite different.

Jeff could have simply decreed that such-and-such a time after dinner is "study hall" in the girls' room and after that is fun time. This would have satisfied his wish to improve Sylvia's study habits, which aren't the best. However, he wisely kept off that topic, realizing that, especially coming on the heels of Sasha's self-righteous criticism of Sylvia's work ethic, it would be counterproductive. He knows that the "why can't you be more like your sister?" discourse will invite more resistance than compliance. Instead, he went right to step one and got them to Talk and Acknowledge. He really had to press hard to get them to restate one another's positions in full detail and without the sarcastic asides.

Jeff made good use of the Parking Lot, letting Sylvia know they would deal with the Eva issue later and then coming back to it as promised. He also used the Lot for his own purposes, going back to something he had seen on Sylvia's face when Sasha first mentioned privacy. Paying close attention to facial reactions and body language really matters. Jeff trusted his intuition and followed through on Sylvia's non-verbal indication of hurt. This turned out to yield a rich lode of feelings to unearth and examine. For one thing, all three of them got an opportunity to explore the relationship shift: whereas Sasha and Sylvia had always gotten on each other's nerves from time to time like any siblings, this was now a matter of *teen privacy* — a different issue. What Jeff shared from his own childhood was well-timed, brief and appropriate. Kids, and teenagers in particular, tend to be allergic to parents' reminiscences of the "I had to walk three miles in the snow uphill both ways" variety. However, his poignant and timely anecdote demonstrated that he *really had been there himself*. He wasn't blaming or proposing a solution or trying to teach anyone a lesson. Personal anecdotes, if used sparingly, can sometimes telegraph empathy more than vague acknowledgments like "I understand" or "This must be so hard for you." His story had the unexpected effect of acting as a softener. Sasha has become somewhat self-absorbed, which is developmentally appropriate for a young teen. Jeff's anecdote helped her to step out of her bubble and to experience a sense of what Sylvia was going through. This might have been what motivated her to offer to take Sylvia shopping. And this happened without overt prompting or coercion. (Imagine how it would have gone over if Jeff or the girls' mother had ordered Sasha to drag Sylvia along to the mall.) This way, Sylvia gets to feel honored, and Sasha gets to feel generous. That's a win/win.

Jeff upheld the "respect" ground rule only when the girls were directly addressing one another. He had them restate sarcastic remarks when necessary. But he chose his battles and was willing to overlook (and not get annoyed by) some problems of tone. For example, when Sasha sarcastically threw out her laundry room idea, he simply took this as a cue to move on to the Brainstorm phase, conveying the sense that, if they tried, they could probably come up with an even better idea. His gentle prompt for Sylvia to reframe her question about Eva was right on the money. Changing "Why can't I meet her?" to "Can I meet her?" made a world of difference. The first version was negative and accusatory, assuming the worst. The second edition sounded neutral, relieved of its baggage.

Jeff bent the rules about keeping Brainstorm separate from mulling the idea over." The contrast between Sylvia's childlike enthusiasm and Sasha's blasé skepticism (both developmentally appropriate) is pretty sharp. Sasha can knock down pins as fast as Sylvia can set them up! However, Sylvia is a nimble thinker, and it was clear to Jeff that she found this challenge bracing rather than daunting. He allowed her upbeat persistence to keep the mediation afloat.

Jeff doesn't believe in forcing his kids to apologize (more about apologies in Chapter Nine.) However, he strongly values a heartfelt apology and wants his kids to as well. He understands that when someone digs deep to come up with an apology and it goes unnoticed, this can be humiliating to the apologizer. And he recognizes that graciously acknowledging an apology is just as much a strategic tool in conflict as being able to apologize. Sylvia's "I'm sorry" to Sasha was openhearted, spontaneous, and authentic. Not wanting the apology to fall flat, Jeff indicated that it deserved some acknowledgment. His prompt required only that; he said nothing about *accepting* the apology or forgiveness. Sasha's acknowledgment was mild but respectful. Both the apology and the acknowledgment may have acted as softeners in the mediation process.

This mediation took a lot of time, the better part of a half hour. It had a lot of parts — some emotional, some practical. For Jeff, the takeaways were threefold. Afterward, chuckling to himself over Sylvia's mom-ish remarks about Sasha's new friend ("We don't even *know* this person Eva!"), he realized that there was some wisdom in Sylvia's concern. Parents should know who their thirteen-year-olds are hanging out with — and thanks to Sylvia's curiosity, the family was on its way to addressing that gap. The second takeaway occurred to him later, while talking things over with the girls' mother. The old, chronic concern about Sylvia's work habits resurfaced. They agreed that this was their challenge to solve — and they determined to tackle this matter with Sylvia while keeping Sasha out of the mix as much as possible. The third takeaway was more personal. Before going to bed, Jeff wrote a rambling, affectionate email to his brother Robert.

# MEDIATION SCENARIO 3

## Mediation in Miniature – The Reframe

Helen has just returned from the mall where she and her two boys have spent several difficult hours that culminated in the full-blown meltdown of her two-year-old son, Amos, over a trinket he wanted and which she refused to buy. "How was the shopping expedition?" her husband asks cheerfully. Before she can find the words to describe her ordeal, four-and-a-half-year-old Alex launches into his own version of the morning's highlight.

Alex: It was awful! Amos is such a baby. Next time we should leave him home!

Helen: (Sinking into a chair) It sounds like you were really bothered by what Amos did.

Alex: (To his dad) He wouldn't stop crying. He was rolling around on the floor of Gemstore. People were staring and pointing. There was all this junk coming out of his nose. He's such a baby.

Helen: I remember how you were looking and acting while

Amos kicked and screamed. I think maybe you were embarrassed by his behavior. Is that right? (Alex doesn't contradict her, so she continues.) Instead of calling him a name, can you tell him how you felt, and tell him what he did that you didn't like?

Alex: Amos, I felt embarrassed when you ... (he's stuck)

Helen: ... were crying?

Alex: ... were crying and rolling around at Gemstore with junk coming out of your nose.

Helen: Thanks, Alex. Now Amos knows *exactly* what he did that you didn't like, and he knows *exactly* how it made you feel.

### THE REFRAME DECONSTRUCTED

Amos has listened sulkily but of course didn't respond. Perhaps he's absorbing what was just said about his behavior and how it affected the older brother he adores and admires. Kudos to Helen for taking the time for this reframe after her grueling morning. It would have been tempting to shoot back with something like, "Well, Alex, calling him a mean name just makes him feel worse — and besides, he practically *is* a baby!"

This whole reframe took less than a minute. Of course it is not a true mediation because the communication is one-way only. However, both children benefited. Amos isn't quite verbal enough to mediate, but hearing reframes and having adults insist that he be addressed respectfully are things that prepare him to problem-solve someday soon. Helen got Alex to focus sharply on two things: the behavior he didn't like and the emotional impact of that behavior on him. In other words, she got him to re-package a grouchy, insulting rant into an I-message. In very short order, Helen has killed four birds with one stone. First, she has let Alex know that she feels name-calling is unacceptable — and pretty ineffectual. Second, she has validated his feelings about the whole episode. Third, she has helped him to articulate these feelings to his brother. Finally, she has seen to it that Alex give Amos something to work with — by trading shaming language for useful and important information to mull over.

# MEDIATION SCENARIO 4

## The Dress-Up Drawer

Madeline is a nurse who gets off work at 3 PM. It's been a very long day, and there's more to come. She picked up her eight-year-old daughter, Laila, at school, and together they drove to the preschool where three-and-a-half-year-old Lewis was just waking up from his nap. Laila spotted Terri, her favorite teacher from back in the day when she attended Lewis' school, and she ran over for a hug. Terri had set up a little circle and was reading to the kids who were already awake. Laila wanted to stay and hear, for the millionth time, what Mr. Bear thinks Danny should give his mother for her birthday. But Madeline explained that they were in a hurry to get home so she could make dinner, because Aunt Ruthie and Uncle Jason are coming for dinner.

While Madeline was getting dinner started in kitchen, Laila set up a reading circle in the hallway next to a big drawer which the kids use for dress-up clothes — a hodgepodge of recycled Halloween costumes, thrift store finery, and clothes their parents have relinquished. Laila, wearing a long skirt that used to be her mom's, has read *Ask Mr. Bear* to Lewis and a collection of dolls she had arranged in the circle. She insisted that Lewis wear a baby bib and call her Miss Terri.

Now Laila is about to launch into *Where the Wild Things Are* when Lewis jumps up and starts rummaging around in the drawer. He puts on one of his father's old neckties over the bib and announces, "I wanna be the Daddy." Laila begins to wail and call for their mother.

Madeline is torn. She wants to get the spaghetti sauce started, but she can hear disaster brewing in the hallway. The last couple of times she let things slide, one of the kids ended up hurting the other. She reasons that if she's probably going to have to get involved anyway, it might as well be to mediate as to fetch bandages and administer discipline. She turns off the burner and throws a tea towel over the half-chopped vegetables just as her kids come thundering into the room. Seeing Lewis wearing the necktie over the bib, it's all she can do not to laugh out loud.

Lewis: (With heat) I wanna be the Daddy!

Laila: (Wailing even louder) It's not fair! We're playing preschool! We're not playing house! He can't be the Daddy!

Madeline: Whoa, slow down. Let's go sit down over here and talk things over. We're going to use our regular voices. We're going to talk, and we're going to listen. Both of you will have a chance to be heard, and both of you can say what you want to say. No yelling, and no mean words. We're going to try really hard to solve this. Are you with me?

Laila: Yes!

Madeline: Lewis, can you agree to those ground rules?

Lewis: (A little guardedly) OK ...

Madeline: Who wants to go first?

Lewis: I wanna be the Daddy!

Madeline: You guys are playing pretend, and you want to be the Daddy. Talk about that a little bit.

Lewis: Daddy goes work. Daddy's big!

Madeline: Laila, what's Lewis saying?

Laila: He wants to be the Daddy. But Mommy, we're not playing *house*!

Madeline: Laila, you know you're going to have your very own turn in a few minutes. Right now it's time to tell us what Lewis said. What did he say?

Laila: (Glumly) He wants to be the Daddy ...

Madeline: And Lewis said he wants to be the Daddy because ...

Laila: Um ... daddies go to work. He said Daddy is big.

Madeline: Thanks! Lewis, did she hear your words?

Lewis: Um, yeah ...

Madeline: So, Laila, what's going on for you?

Laila: We're playing *preschool*. I'm pretending to be Miss Terri. I read *Ask Mr. Bear*. I started to read *Where the Wild Things Are*, but then Lewis wouldn't play anymore.

Madeline: How did that make you feel?

Laila: Mad. Mad and sad ...

Madeline: It's kind of frustrating when you have an idea of

how to play and the other person doesn't want to play anymore ... and it's discouraging when the other person quits and you're not ready to be done. Lewis, what has Laila been saying?

Lewis: She wants to be Miss Terri and read to me. I don't wanna play preschool anymore. I wanna be the Daddy!

Madeline: Um, Lewis, how did Laila say this is making her *feel*?

Lewis: Mad.

Laila: And frustrated.

Lewis: And fluster-ated.

Laila: (Insistently) Frustrated!

Lewis: Frus ... (he gives up)

Laila: (Slowly, carefully) Frus-tra-ted!

Lewis: Frus-tra-ted ...

Madeline: Laila, did Lewis hear your words?

Laila: Yeah.

Madeline: So does anyone have an idea how you can solve this problem?

Lewis: I wanna be the Daddy!

Madeline: That's one idea. Laila, do you have any ideas?

Laila: We could play library. I could be Ms. Patterson and you (indicated her brother) could be one of the kids at Storytime. The dolls can be the other kids.

Lewis: But I wanna be the Daddy!

Madeline: OK, we have two ideas. Lewis wants to be a Daddy and Laila suggests you guys play library. (Glancing at the bib, suppressing a smile) It looks like Lewis played baby for a while and now he wants to play a grownup. I heard him say "Daddy is big!"

Laila: But it's not fair for him to stop in the middle! We were playing preschool, and then he jumped up and now everything is spoiled. (She begins to well up with tears.)

Madeline: You were having so much fun being Miss Terri. You really love her! You were using your imagination to pretend to be Miss Terri. You got to read one of your favorite books to the kids, just like she does. And Lewis was using his imagination to pretend to be a little tiny kid. Now he wants to use his imagination to be a Daddy.

Laila: It's not fair!

Madeline: At our house, what's fair is that everybody gets to be in charge of their own imagination. That means you can pretend to be anyone you want to be, and Lewis can pretend to be anyone he wants to be. I think our job is to find something fun to play where each of you can pretend to be who you want to be.

Laila: I want to read *Where the Wild Things Are*!

Lewis: We could play Go to the Park ...

Madeline: We have a lot of suggestions. Lewis wants to be the Daddy. Laila wants to read *Where the Wild Things Are*. We have a suggestion about playing library, and we have a suggestion about playing Go to the Park. (There is a very long pause. Madeline sits back and takes her time, looking intently at one child, then the other.)

Laila: (Thinking hard) Daddies go to the library ...

Madeline: Aha!

Laila: Raj and Shareen's daddy takes them to Storytime. I can be Ms. Patterson and read *Where the Wild Things Are*. Lewis, you could be Raj and Shareen's daddy. You could wear one of my dolls in the backpack to be Shareen — and another dolly can sit on your lap and be Raj! (Eagerly) I'll go get our old backpack out of the dress-up drawer ...

Lewis: But I wanna be *our* Daddy! (There is a long silence while Laila takes this in. She looks crestfallen.)

Madeline: Oh, wow, you guys were *so close* to getting to a solution! Any idea how this could work? With Lewis pretending to be his own Daddy?

Laila: My Daddy too!

Madeline: Yes, your Daddy too — of course.

Laila: (Light bulb moment) The doll in the backpack can be Baby Lewis and the doll in his lap can be me! Like a long time ago, when Daddy used to take us to Storytime at the library.

Lewis: I don't remember ...

Laila: No, because you were the baby. In the backpack. Get it?

Lewis: (Tentatively) I think so … (Madeline can see that he doesn't get it at all.)

Madeline: Hold on, I'm going to get a picture. (She goes into the living room and comes back with a small framed photograph she took several years ago on a family hike. It's a picture of her husband holding Laila's hand, with Lewis in a backpack.) Here, you guys, sit together on the couch so you can both see. (Madeline lets the kids take their time poring over the picture together.)

Lewis: (Pointing to his baby self in the picture) That's me!

Madeline: That's right … and who is that little girl in the picture?

Lewis and Laila (In unison): Laila!!

Madeline: Lewis, when I took this picture, you were a little baby, and Laila was about the age you are now.

Lewis: (Gazes at the picture for a long while, then brightens) I wanna be the Daddy!

Laila: I'll go get the backpack.

Madeline: (Putting a hand on her arm and addressing Lewis) Wait a sec — do we have an agreement?

Lewis: (Explaining patiently to his mother) Yeah! I play the Daddy. Baby Lewis be in the backpack, and I hold Laila in my lap. And she (indicating his sister) play Ms. Patterson.

Laila: And I'll read *Where the Wild Things Are*.

Lewis: Wild Things!

Madeline: Great job, guys ... thanks.

## The Dress-Up Drawer Mediation Deconstructed

Later, stirring the spaghetti sauce, Madeline had time to think about how the mediation went. It had been hard, from the beginning, to get each child to hear the other. Madeline had to be very insistent, and provide a lot of expressive language, before her kids could accurately re-state one another's position. But her biggest challenge was power-balancing. With all the single-mindedness of a preschooler, Lewis kept up the same refrain throughout — "I wanna be the Daddy!" Madeline chose to honor this as a suggestion. Laila, being older, is shrewder than Lewis, and her first solution was simply to export the game from the classroom to the library. This would have preserved the power relationship of playing preschool, with Laila as the authority figure and Lewis as a little kid. Madeline knew this wouldn't satisfy Lewis' wish to be big, so she elaborated for the kids' benefit: "It looks like Lewis played baby for a while, and now he wants to play a grownup. I heard him say 'Daddy is big!'" Restating what Lewis said had the effect of amplifying his wants so that Laila could better understand him. In this way, Madeline could bring clarity without appearing to take sides and without overt persuasion.

And when Laila complained that it wasn't fair for Lewis to quit mid-game, Madeline first provided some Active Listening that Lewis couldn't. By responding warmly to Laila's feelings about Ms. Terri and the fun of impersonating her, she helped Laila "feel felt": "You were having so much fun being Ms. Terri. You really love her! You were using your imagination to pretend to be Miss Terri. You got to read one of your favorite books to the kids, just like she does. And Lewis was using his imagination to pretend to be a little tiny kid. Now he wants to use his imagination to be a daddy." This may have acted as a softener for what followed, but it was by no means a wave of the magic wand, because her daughter's response was simply to repeat, "It's not fair." Laila was stuck.

At this point, Madeline did an interesting thing. She stepped out of her mediator role to state a family rule: "At our house, what's fair is that everybody gets to be in charge of their own imagination. That means you can pretend to be anyone you want to be, and Lewis can pretend to be anyone he wants to be." Short and sweet, her two-sentence observation provided a rule and an interpretation.

By stating and clarifying the family rule, she spotlighted the disciplinary umbrella that hovers over every family mediation, saying, in effect, *I will be neutral about what you two decide to do as long as it doesn't violate the law of the land, which I'm obligated to uphold.* Then she jumped right back into mediator mode: "I think our job is to find something fun to play where each of you can pretend to be who you want to be." (For more about the interplay between mediation and discipline, see Mediation Scenario 8 and the beginning of Chapter Six.)

Laila, however, wasn't sold on the idea. Still stuck, she simply restated that she wanted to read *Where the Wild Things Are*. This jogged the park idea from Lewis. Doggedly, Madeline treated all of these as plausible suggestions: being daddy ... reading *Where The Wild Things Are* ... playing library ... playing park. This paid off when Laila began to hybridize the ideas with, "Daddies go to the library ... "

Things almost broke down when Lewis didn't accept his sister's elaborate idea about which daddy he should portray at "her" library. Here Madeline stepped in as cheerleader, at the same time providing reinforcement of the family rule governing imagination: "Oh, wow, you guys were *so close* to getting to a solution! Any idea how this could work? With Lewis pretending to be his own Daddy?"

This led to an unexpected trip down memory lane, with Laila as tour guide. Madeline supported this process with the photograph she showed them. She was power-balancing here, because Laila's grasp of the scenario left Lewis in the dust. The photo gave Lewis something concrete to latch onto so he could "get it" ... *Daddy used to take us to Storytime when I was just a tiny baby in a backpack and Laila was the age I am now!* Seating her children side-by-side to look at the photo was a good strategy. It can feel more like a partnership to sit shoulder to shoulder with someone: *It's you and me against the problem.*

Madeline took a final moment to goof-proof, making certain that Lewis understood the game they were going to play and approved his role in it. His answer indicated both: "I play the Daddy. Baby Lewis be in the backpack, and I hold Laila in my lap. And she [indicating his sister] play Ms. Patterson." Once Laila reiterated her wish to read "Wild Things" and got buy-in from Lewis, they were good to go.

# MEDIATION SCENARIO 5

## Talk to the Door

Joshua (17) and Rachel (15) are pretty typical teenagers. Both good students, they are busy kids, with friends to see and numerous extra-curriculars to round out their days. Their parents are divorced, so they live with their mom, Adrienne, Monday through Thursday, and they spend weekends with their dad, Howard. Lately there has been a lot of heat and commotion in the kids' relationship, so much so that Howard has suggested re-designing their living arrangements so that they don't spend so much time in the same household. Howard makes a pretty convincing case: if he had Joshua for half the week and Rachel on the other days (and if Adrienne's schedule with the kids were the reverse) he and his son would have more man-to-man time at this critical stage of life — and both Howard and Adrienne would be spared all the drama of two teenagers under the same roof. Although the vision of peaceful alone time with each child is tempting, Adrienne balks at this idea. After all, one of the reasons they had two kids in the first place was so they would learn to play well with others. She remembers how close the children grew during the divorce ... that they were really there for each other. And she senses that, for both kids, having a sibling to transition with as they shuttle between their two households is extremely grounding. But what Adrienne finds most compelling is that, with Joshua starting to look at colleges, he and Rachel really only have another year at home before their lives change forever. It makes her sad to think of the kids' time together under the same roof ending on such a sour note.

It's been a tense week, and Adrienne is frankly looking forward to her weekend alone. Tonight has followed a typical pattern; the kids began fighting over some small thing — Adrienne has no idea how it got started — and then Rachel began screaming at Joshua. In exasperation, he has fled to his room. Now, as usual, Rachel is standing outside his door, yelling and carrying on. In about five minutes, she will tire of this and go back to what she was doing. Adrienne doesn't get involved in these scenes; her kids are way past the age of coming to blows, and these episodes tend to just burn themselves out. Or do they? It's such a persistent pattern. *How did it come to this? Why are they stuck?* she wonders, not for the first time.

Something has to be done. Not having the slightest idea how to proceed, but feeling that there's very little to lose, Adrienne goes into the hall. She puts a finger to her lips. Rachel stops in mid-rant, rather surprised to see her mom intervene.

Adrienne: I think we should talk.

Rachel: (At the top of her voice) He's the one you should be talking to …

Adrienne: (Very, very quietly) I said *talk*. Not yell. I want to talk with both of you.

Rachel: He won't come out.

Adrienne: Can you go wait for us in the living room? I'll see what I can do … no guarantees. (Rachel snorts petulantly and saunters off to the living room. Adrienne takes a deep breath, rolls her shoulders a few times, and knocks loudly on the door.) Joshua?

Joshua: (Very grumpily) Yeah? Mom?

Adrienne: Josh, I think you and Rachel and I need to talk.

Joshua: (After a long, long silence.) There's no point.

Adrienne: There's always a point. We're a *fam* —

Joshua: (Grouchier still) You don't get it! She's a drama queen! She *likes* all the fighting and screaming!

Adrienne: (Pause) Well, *I* don't. Do you? Wouldn't you like to see if you could get it to stop?

Joshua: I do get it to stop. I come in here, put on my headphones, and it stops.

Adrienne: It doesn't stop for me!

Joshua: Get headphones!

Adrienne: Joshua, can I please come in? It's hard to have this conversation through the door!

Joshua: (Another long silence, followed by a loud, dramatic sigh.) OK, I guess. (Adrienne enters his inner sanctum gingerly and perches at the foot of his bed, where he is slouching over a calculus text. He is wearing the same look of dread he used to have as a small child when he had to go to the doctor for his yearly physical. How this boy hates being *probed.*) I don't have much time.

Adrienne: I understand. Half hour max. (He winces.) OK, twenty minutes. Please let's give this thing a chance. You don't have to believe it will work. *I'm* not even sure it will work. All

I ask is that you try. (He is unmoved; she can see it.) Please, twenty minutes?

Joshua: (Clearly, this is almost physically painful for him. He just wants the talking to stop.) OK, but *twenty minutes*. (He sets the timer on his cell, shoots his mom a dire look, and stands up. They join Rachel in the living room.)

Adrienne: So ... what we're going to do here is we're going to talk, and we're going to listen. I'm going to try to stay in the middle and not take sides. My job is to try to ask good questions. I'm not going to advise you or make any suggestions. OK?

Joshua: This is weird ...

Adrienne: Yes it is ... I know ... (*now* he's paying attention!) So I need you both to talk in a regular voice, no yelling. I want to have a respectful conversation — without sarcasm or eye-rolling or any of that. Are you in? (They shift uncomfortably, mumbling assent.) OK, so I was noticing that you were yelling, Rachel. Can you tell Joshua what was bothering you?

Rachel: We were fighting about something, and like always, he just left.

Adrienne: Joshua, what's bothering Rachel?

Joshua: (Looking at his Mom as if she has rocks in her head) She just *told* us!

Adrienne: Yes, and now I'd like you to restate what she said.

Joshua: (Glancing at his cell) *Eighteen minutes*, Mom!

Adrienne: What did she say?

Joshua: She said we were fighting, and I left.

Adrienne: Yes, exactly, thank you. Rachel, how do you feel when he leaves?

Rachel: So mad. I want to scream.

Joshua: You *do* scream. You scream a lot!

Adrienne: (Seeing that Rachel is starting to flare; perhaps some venting would help.) So Rachel, talk a bit more about that. How does it feel when you want to have it out with Joshua and he leaves?

Rachel: Just ... so ... (she makes a clenching, shivering gesture and nearly growls.)

Adrienne: Frustrated?

Joshua: Hey, you're putting words in her mouth!

Adrienne: Sorry, Josh but it sure looked like frustration to me. Would you like to ask her how she feels when you leave? Maybe I've got it wrong. (She looks back and forth between the two kids.)

Joshua: OK, fine, she gets frustrated.

Adrienne: Any other feelings, Rachel?

Rachel: (Who has calmed down considerably, if her body language is any indication) I don't know, it's like I'm not even important enough, like I'm not worth his time ...

Adrienne: (Not about to make the mistake again!) Josh, how would you describe that feeling?

Joshua: (After a thoughtful pause) Maybe ... disrespected?

Rachel: Yes! Frustrated and disrespected! When you get up and leave ...

Adrienne: Thank you both. It really helps us all to know how that makes you feel, Rachel. Now Joshua, you've been really patient, and we have only — (indicating his cell phone, smiling)

Joshua: (Consulting the cell) Fifteen minutes —

Adrienne: — Fifteen minutes left. So Josh, what's bothering you about this situation?

Joshua: The yelling. I really hate yelling.

Adrienne: How does yelling make you feel?

Joshua: Um, I dunno, bad. C'mon, no one likes to be yelled at!

Adrienne: (After a pause, gently) This is torture, isn't it?

Joshua: Huh?

Adrienne: Being asked to take out your feelings and talk about them? (He squirms.) It's a big concession for you even to agree to do this. I appreciate it. (She shoots a quick look at Rachel.)

Rachel: Me too.

Adrienne: (After waiting a few beats to let this sink in.) So ... I'm guessing that the yelling makes you feel like escaping ... just doing anything to flee the scene. (He nods.) So what do you guys think we can do to solve the problem?

Rachel: If he would just stay and *talk* ...

Joshua: But you *don't* talk, Raych! (Adrienne can't help noticing that he used his sister's nickname.) You go right into screaming mode —

Rachel: I get excited! Maybe I raise my voice when I get excited ...

Joshua: Why do you have to call it "raising your voice?" You were yelling!

Adrienne: Rachel, would you feel better about this discussion if we call it "raising your voice"?

Rachel: Well, OK, so in the living room I was raising my voice. When you went to your room and shut me out, I started yelling.

Adrienne: So Rachel, arguing with Joshua made you raise your voice, and when he left the room to escape, you started yelling.

Rachel: Exactly.

Joshua: OK, so fine. When we're arguing and you "raise your voice," all I want is to escape! Seriously, Raych, I would stay and talk if we could be quiet and logical ... (Rachel humphs.)

Adrienne: Rachel, please remember we agreed to keep this respectful. (Brightening) So ,I heard a suggestion and a counter-suggestion. Joshua, you want Rachel to keep her voice down when the two of you have a conflict. Rachel, you want Joshua to stay and talk it out. Could you guys do that?

Rachel: Yes! (Joshua is looking extremely skeptical.)

Joshua: I'll spend like ten minutes, but I'm not into long talks that take all night. I'm really pressured with college apps and everything. (Adrienne notices Rachel's posture sag.)

Adrienne: What happens if Rachel's not raising her voice but the ten minutes are up?

Rachel: Can we stop where we are and pick it up again later? Like maybe the next day? (At this, Joshua starts to look aggrieved.)

Adrienne: Josh, we know that talking things out isn't your cup of tea. At this point, I'd like you to think about how much you are willing to concede to make the yelling stop. (This is a tough sell.) Let's say you're having an argument with Rachel and she raises her voice. What is your recourse?

Rachel: He could say he doesn't want to talk with me when I'm raising my voice.

Adrienne: And then what?

Joshua: I could just ... stop. And leave.

Rachel: Fine.

Adrienne: And you wouldn't start yelling if he left, Rachel? (Rachel shakes her head "no" emphatically.) That's a big commitment. Do you think you can keep control of your voice, even when you guys are having a big disagreement?

Rachel: I'll try.

Adrienne: And you'll pay the price if you lose control? (Rachel nods.) OK, Joshua, are you willing to put in ten minutes, even several nights running if necessary, in the interest of having a

— what did you say, Joshua? "quiet and logical"? — discussion?

Joshua: Yeah, I guess so.

Adrienne: Great! How much more time do we have?

Josh: (Glancing at his cell) Three minutes!

Adrienne: (Wryly) You're off the hook. Thanks, guys, good work. Let's remember to fill your Dad in about this agreement when I drop you off tomorrow.

### TALK TO THE DOOR MEDIATION DECONSTRUCTED

From the get-go, Adrienne was under extraordinary pressure because of the time constraint. However, setting a time limit was her only bargaining chip in getting Joshua "to the table," and she made the best of it. Like a lot of parents who haven't been mediating since the kids were small, she has a lot of awkwardness and skepticism to overcome ... her own as well as theirs. However, she was fiercely determined to get them to mediate. She skillfully avoided their attempts to engage her in a "discussion before the discussion," insisting that mediation would be the best way to address their respective grievances. (See "Don't Let the Mediation Start Without You," Chapter Six.)

Getting the kids to Talk and Acknowledge wasn't easy, but she kept firm control of the conversation. When Joshua reacted negatively to Adrienne's offer of an interpretation ("frustrated?") to Rachel, she backed off, indicating that it was just a guess and maybe an incorrect one. (Active Listening by the mediator often strikes parties who are new to mediation as taking sides.) Soon after, she offered Joshua the opportunity to come up with the next interpretation ("disrespected") and this paid off. After all, he is a smart kid with a great vocabulary, so Adrienne created an opportunity for him to demonstrate his empathy to Rachel.

Joshua's resistance to talking about his feelings colored this whole mediation. Adrienne's decision to address his resistance head-on was a good strategy. The timing was good too, her manner understanding and non-judgmental. Adrienne gets it that Rachel is never happier than when she's sharing feelings. Like a lot of teenage girls, she's constantly texting and chatting about this friend or that, scrutinizing their relationships and conversations, mining them for deep meaning. Joshua, like most males, is disinclined to perform these relational autopsies. The mediation *itself* puts Rachel at an advantage and Joshua at a disadvantage. Adrienne was doing (perhaps unconsciously) some power-balancing. In acknowledging that Joshua has already made a huge concession by stepping out of his comfort zone in order to mediate, she subtly pointed out to her daughter that Rachel had already earned a take-away even before the real bargaining began. That prompted Rachel to thank him also. (This acted as a softener; Adrienne couldn't help noticing that the next time Joshua addressed Rachel, he used the family's affectionate nickname for her.) Adrienne also helped him amplify his reaction. He said yelling made him feel "bad," which is not a very powerful or expressive word. Adrienne turned up the heat with "escape" and "like fleeing." These words are not only more pungent, but they also more accurately describe his reaction, which is to bolt to the sanctuary of his room.

Adrienne let Rachel have her way about the terms "raising her voice" and "yelling." Being allowed to define behavior in her own words meant that Rachel could save face and move on. Insisting on certain language that one or both parties find offensive or inaccurate can derail a mediation.

Adrienne, no doubt feeling the time crunch, rushed straight in and out of the brainstorming phase: "So I heard a suggestion and a counter-suggestion." She was lucky here because the two offers were fairly symmetrical, and because they wouldn't cancel each other out. (This was pure luck. Often, at the outset of a conflict, two parties will take positions that are mutually exclusive, as in "I need the computer" versus "No, *I* need the computer.") She jumped right on it, but was careful to goof-proof with a "what if" question. Here, the goof-proofing actually provided some assurances to Joshua, who was still balky about signing on. He got a promise that if Rachel were to default on her part of the bargain, then he would be completely free to leave without triggering a yelling episode.

Exhausted but feeling a sense of accomplishment, Adrienne smiled to herself and thought, *Well, that was seventeen minutes well-spent.*

# MEDIATION SCENARIO 6

## A Multiparty Dispute: "Gimme the Remote"

Linda and her husband Jeff have been mediating with their three children since the kids were small. Just as Jeff is finishing the dinner dishes and Linda sits down to pay some bills, a conflict of epic proportion breaks out in the family room. All three children are hollering. Her youngest, Marcus, seven, is in tears. He and Denise, nine, are trying to get the remote from Albert, who is fourteen. Being a head taller than the other two, Albert is playing keep-away by dangling the remote high above their heads. The two younger children are leaping and snapping like terriers to get at the precious electronic grail.

> Linda: (Walking into the family room) Good Lord! What's this all about? Everybody looks very, very angry and upset. I think we all need to sit down and talk this through. You know the ground rules, right? (They all nod and settle in.) OK, thank you. Marcus, I see that you're crying. What's going on?

> Marcus: (Through his tears, hiccuping) Albert said I'm immature!

Albert: Well, he *is*. I mean look at him!

Linda: Albert, it's not unusual for a child seven years younger than you to be less mature than you are. But in this case the word "immature" sounds kind of like an insult. Marcus, is that how it felt to you?

Marcus: (With indignation) Yes! I'm not a baby, I'm almost eight!

Denise: (Primly) I think Albert should apologize. (All eyes fall on Albert.)

Albert: (Quietly, in Marcus' general direction) Sorry.

Linda: OK, so what's going on here?

Albert: OK, so I'm supposed to watch "Creatures of the Deep" in a half hour. It's for my science class. I have to hand in a three-paragraph review of the show tomorrow.

Marcus: What's a paragraph? (Albert huffs in exasperation and turns away.)

Linda: (To Marcus) We'll put that in the Parking Lot. (To Albert) Do we need to go over the ground rules? *Respect?* (Albert squirms, adjusts his posture.)

Linda: (To the younger two) So what's going on for Albert?

Denise: He has to watch the show at 7:30. It's for school.

Linda: Anything else?

Marcus: He'll be in trouble if he doesn't hand in ... that thing ... tomorrow.

Linda: That's right, you two. And what's going on for you?

Denise: Marcus and I were arguing over the remote when Albert came in and grabbed it.

Albert: I tried to explain why I needed it, but they were already so upset they wouldn't listen!

Linda: How did it make you feel when Albert grabbed the remote?

Denise: Frustrated!

Marcus: So mad!

Linda: Albert, could you recap that?

Albert: When I grabbed the remote, they felt frustrated and angry.

Linda: (To Denise and Marcus) Tell me a little more about your argument.

Denise: We both wanted the remote. It was 7:00 and "Kick the Can" was starting. I didn't want to miss it!

Marcus: (Surprised, to Denise) You wanted to watch "Kick the Can" too?

Albert: Oh man — you guys were fighting over the remote, and it turns out you *both* wanted to watch the *same show*? (Linda lets this light bulb moment sink in.)

Linda: Albert, what do you think they could have done about the remote before all the yelling started?

Albert: They could have talked about what they wanted.

Linda: Good idea. Maybe a lot of fighting could have been avoided. But I've noticed that you two (gesturing the younger ones) often argue over the remote even when you want to watch the same show. There's something about holding the remote that must be very important to both of you that doesn't have anything to do with what show you're watching. Maybe we can park that for a future discussion. Albert, I'm not understanding why you came in at 7:00 if your show begins at 7:30.

Albert: 'Cuz I know that "Kick the Can" is an hour long. If I came in at 7:30 and they were halfway through the show, it would have been World War III!

Linda: So you were planning ahead. For next time, is there maybe a way of planning ahead that's even better?

Denise: We could make a chart!

Albert: I only got this assignment *today*!

Denise: How about ... we talk it over at dinner?

Marcus: Albert never talks at dinner. (Albert's eyes widen a bit at this.)

Linda: Wow, Marcus, "never" is a pretty strong word. It sounds like maybe you'd like to ask Albert something.

Marcus (After a long pause) I want you to talk to us at dinner.

Albert: About what?

Denise: Well, your plans about the TV, for one thing.

Linda: This is getting complicated. (She finds a paper and pencil and begins writing.) Albert, do you think you could agree to that? (He shrugs.) OK, maybe — and there's that Parking Lot thing about what a paragraph is. And some kind of talk between Marcus and Denise about the remote. (There is a long pause. Albert's show is on in fifteen minutes. Should she turn to the matter of Denise and Marcus and the remote?)

Denise: I wish we had a DVR like Allison. Her parents don't like her to watch TV on school nights, so she records stuff and watches it later.

Albert: (Warming to the idea, selling it to Mom, even) And you can skip the commercials, so it actually saves time!

Marcus: I like commercials! (Linda notices that Albert and Denise exchange quick smiles.)

Linda: Dad and I have talked about that. The McClellans have three kids too, and they swear by it. We were actually talking about putting away some money to buy one, and then that car thing happened right after the holidays. We just kind of put it on hold.

Denise: Maybe we need a jar.

Marcus: Why a jar?

Denise: Remember? Last year, our classroom wanted to buy a hamster. Ms. Chin brought in a big jar and put a quarter in. The rule was "pay what you can when you can." In about a month, we had enough money to buy Mr. Potter and a really cool cage. We still use the jar for his food, but now you don't have to put in as much.

Linda: (Noticing that Albert has started to sigh and fidget. He has probably heard the saga of the jar, the cage and Mr. Potter a few times too many.) Well, guys, assuming you were willing to help pay for a DVR — and no one has agreed to that yet, let's be clear — what would be a fair way to divide up the cost? Albert, you're good with numbers, what do you think?

Albert: Well, my allowance is about three times as much as Marcus' and Denise's is twice as much as his. (Everyone reacts to this sudden burst of data.) Well, it's true — I keep track of this stuff! (He pauses to think.) I could probably spare $3.00 a week. If Denise gave $2.00 and Marcus kicked in $1.00, we'd have —

Linda: (Interrupting, putting a hand on Albert's arm) How much, Denise?

Denise: Um ... $6.00!

Marcus: $6.00 a week! How long would it be before we had enough to buy the DVR?

Linda: Well, I can't speak for Dad, but I think he and I can commit to putting some money in every week as well. After all, we watch TV too. Plus the peace and quiet should be well worth it. How about I talk to him, and we'll get back to you with a number?

Denise: Even if you and Dad don't, I want to start a jar.

Albert: I'm in!

Marcus: Me too!

Linda: So what have we got? Um ... Albert, can you agree to be more conversational with the family at dinner?

Albert: Yeah, I guess so.

Linda: (Turning to the younger kids) And right now Albert's going to watch his show, because it's for school. (They nod.) Albert, can you explain what a paragraph is to Marcus sometime? Not right now, your show's almost on.

Albert: Sure.

Linda: When? (Long pause. Albert is stuck.)

Denise: Tomorrow night at dinner?

Albert: Sure.

Linda: Super! And you two (indicating Denise and Marcus) — it's almost bedtime, but I'd like to talk with both of you about the remote tomorrow night right after dinner. Deal? (They nod.)

Linda: OK. I promise Dad and I will talk about the DVR fund and get back to you sometime tomorrow. Thank you guys, good job.

### A Multiparty Dispute Mediation Deconstructed

A multi-party mediation with children of varying ages is always a challenge. Linda has compared it to running a three-ring circus with different size rings. Denise is a typical middle child; she enjoys coming up with suggestions and keeping it together. But it's easy for Linda to lose Albert, the participant at the upper range of maturity, if the conversation gets too simplistic. Likewise, Linda has to take special measures to make sure the discussion doesn't go over the head of Marcus, the youngest (and least mature) party. She began with Marcus because, being the most distraught, he was most in need of calming. Without belaboring the point, she reminded her oldest that *of course* the youngest is, by comparison, immature, but that turning this into an insult is below the belt. By doing what she could to level the playing field from the onset, she got the mediation off to a pretty good start. And she used what mediators call Power Balancing techniques throughout. (More about Power Balancing in Chapter Six.)

This family is quite mediation-savvy. Linda has learned to begin and end each mediation with a simple acknowledgment. By bracketing each discussion in a ritualistic way, she sets a positive intention ("we can do this") and then expresses gratitude ("we did it.") It's important to note that this family is by no means immune to high emotion and disrespectful moments. However, they were able to recover themselves quickly. As psychologists say, rupture was followed by repair (more about this in Chapter Nine.) The three children began working constructively and cooperatively on a solution with relative speed. They are old pros at it. What this means is that they trust the process. Each knew that the investment of time and effort would pay off. Each assumed that there was a high probability of taking away something of value — and they were not disappointed.

Linda has gotten good at reading cues. Albert's immediate, enthusiastic response to Denise's suggestion about the DVR emboldened her to explore the idea further with them (even though, as she cautioned, "no one has agreed to that yet, let's be clear.") A bit later, when Albert's commitment to the process began to flag, she enlisted his math skill as a way of getting him back in the game.

Linda was careful not to commit to the parental share without consulting her husband, Bruce. Although she had a number in mind ($12.00 weekly, double the kids' total) and although she was nearly certain their dad would agree to some level of participation, she promised nothing. If Linda were to offer the kids one amount, and then come back (after talking to Bruce) with a lower amount, she would be setting her husband up as the Bad Guy. This type of goof-proofing protects not only the mediation, but also the mediators.

The mediation provided an unexpected take-away for Linda. Lately, she and Bruce had been grousing to one another about

Albert's demeanor at dinner. Albert was often sulky and distant, but they hadn't yet really taken that bull by the horns. She was floored to learn that it had been bothering Marcus. Who would have guessed he was upset by it too? Linda was glad she had encouraged Marcus to reframe his complaint about Albert ("Albert never talks at dinner") as a request. Albert was utterly disarmed by his little brother; he had agreed to change his behavior almost reflexively. Linda smiled ruefully. She could only imagine the blowback she or Bruce might have gotten with the same request! Well, Albert had insights of his own. She resolved to use his observation ("you guys were fighting over the remote, and it turns out you both wanted to watch the *same show*?") as a springboard for her upcoming discussion with Denise and Marcus about the remote.

# MEDIATION SCENARIO 7

## "The Young and the Restless"

Luis (3) and his little sister Marisela (1½) are playing in the sandbox on the back patio. Their dad, Samuel, has been doing tax returns in the kitchen. He hears a ruckus and heads out to the patio. The scene is almost comical: his two children, surrounded by sand toys and plastic vehicles of every description, are each holding on for dear life to opposite ends of the *same yellow truck*!

> Samuel: (Squatting on the edge of the sandbox) Wow, what's going on here? It looks like you both *really* want that truck! (Both children stop yelling, but they are still tugging on the vehicle.) I think I'm going to hold this while we talk. (He wrests the truck from their hands.) Marisela, I can see from your face that you are very angry and frustrated. It looks like you really want to play with the truck! Do you want to tell Luis that?
>
> Marisela: Me truck!
>
> Luis: *I* want the truck! I had it first!

Samuel: How are you feeling about that?

Luis: I'm mad!

Samuel: I can see how mad you are. Looks like this is frustrating for you, too ...

Luis: Yeah!

Samuel: So let's see ... you're both feeling very angry and frustrated. You both want the yellow truck. I'm wondering how we can work this out ... (He lets this sink in. For a full two minutes, no one says anything. Samuel looks back and forth inquiringly at the two children. He can practically hear the wheels turning.)

Luis: (At last) I want the truck. I had I first!

Marisela: Me! Me truck! (She lunges angrily at her brother.)

Samuel: Marisela, I'm going to hold on to you so no one gets hurt. (He places the truck behind him and arranges Marisela in his lap, facing Luis) I get it! Both of you really want the truck, and you are both really angry and really frustrated.

Luis: (After another pause) Me first?

Samuel: You first ... and then what?

Luis: Then Marisela.

Samuel: I see. You want to take turns. That's an interesting idea. Marisela, do you think taking turns is a good idea? (She nods solemnly.) Luis, how would that work?

Luis: I get it, and then she gets it.

Samuel: How many minutes will you need with it?

Luis: (Holding up all ten fingers) This many!

Samuel: OK, so you want it for ten minutes, and then you'll give it to Marisela? And then Marisela can play with it *all by herself*? (He turns to Marisela when he says this, trying to make it sound delicious.)

Luis: Yes.

Samuel: Marisela, how does that sound to you? Ten minutes and then you can play with the truck all by yourself? (She nods.) OK, it's a deal. It's 10:30, and Luis will give you the truck at 10:40. (He sets his phone to beep.) Thanks, you two ...

Samuel followed through, and this meant investing time he would otherwise have used to finish his chores. Really wanting the resolution to stick, he sat with the kids in the sandbox while Luis had his ten minutes with the truck. A few times during this eternity, Marisela approached her Dad, whining about the truck and pointing indignantly at Luis. Instead of moralizing, Samuel offered empathy and encouragement: "It's so hard to wait. Ten minutes feels like a very long time when you really want something a lot. I bet you're really going to enjoy having the truck all to yourself. Only three more minutes to go!" He remembered to give Luis a one-minute warning when his turn was winding down and made sure that Luis handed the truck to his sister in respectful completion of his portion of the contract. Samuel thanked Luis for the hand-off and acknowledged Marisela for waiting.

### "THE YOUNG AND THE RESTLESS" MEDIATION DECONSTRUCTED

For starters, kudos to Samuel for not making Luis relinquish the truck to his little sister. This just breeds resentment and teaches older siblings to be sneaky (more about this in Chapter Nine, "Is Sharing a

'Should'?") Keeping in mind that his daughter is barely verbal, Samuel power-balanced by addressing her first, reading her face for clues and providing her with emotion words. Giving her words also served to model some language for Luis. By getting the mediation off to an empathetic but businesslike start, he signaled the children that no amount of over-dramatic carrying on would win the day.

Samuel knew this would have to be short and sweet. His kids are very young, with limited vocabularies and even more limited attention spans. He respected their need for a simple, speedy process. He could see that they were both feeling angry and frustrated, and he said so. He knows that both children are still so young that, developmentally, they are self-absorbed — and appropriately so. But he also knows that it's never too early to plant a seed of empathy. After all, the emotions that had seized Luis were exactly mirrored in Marisela. This was certainly worth their consideration.

By going right to the heart of an "I want it" / "No, I want it" dispute, Samuel wasn't just stating the obvious or wasting time. He let them say what he knew perfectly well they would say, and allowed it to linger in the air. This created some space in which the kids could ponder the puzzle. In the deep, long silence, both Luis and Marisela experienced a "light bulb moment": *We both want sole possession of the exact same thing. Neither of us can be 100 percent happy with the outcome.* And that in itself is huge.

Samuel was listening very, very carefully. Luis' first suggestion ("I want the truck") was not conciliatory at all. It was just a restatement of his position. But his next gambit ("Me first?") hinted at taking turns, and Samuel helped him flesh out this idea. Samuel allowed Luis to invent the idea of taking turns, showing interest in the idea but without acting as though Luis had gotten the one right answer. Although Luis' solution was very much like the one most adults would arbitrate, getting to the solution independently and having his sister agree to it were powerful experiences for Luis. And Marisela had a choice about agreeing to her brother's suggestion. Having a choice feels very different from having to resign oneself to an adult's arbitrated decision.

It's usually not a good idea to physically side with one child during mediation (for example, snuggling with one or sitting a lot closer to one than the other.) But in this case, holding Marisela proved necessary — and Samuel's words helped Luis understand that his Dad was not showing favoritism but rather keeping him (Luis) physically safe: "Marisela, I'm going to hold on to you so no one gets hurt."

Samuel realized that without follow-through, everything could have *fallen* through. You don't build a gorgeous wooden tree house and not protect it with varnish or paint. The structure would crumble, and all your effort would be for nothing. Samuel protected the process he'd invested in (the mediation) by investing further (follow-through.)

# MEDIATION SCENARIO 8

## Compound Fracture

Toby (6) and Zach (5) have been out in the backyard looking for bugs — their current passion. Their mom, Masako, is spending her Saturday morning getting caught up on household chores. After about an hour, it occurs to her how well the boys have been getting along, playing independently without the need for her constant intervention. No sooner has she flushed with pleasure at this realization than she hears a terrible commotion. Now the noise is getting closer. Toby appears in the doorway, holding his arm gingerly, tears streaming down his face. "Zach pushed me off the swing," he howls indignantly. Zach is hard on Toby's heels, already spouting excuses.

"Zach," Masako says sternly, "Please get me an ice pack from the freezer." She sits with her arm around Toby, examining his arm by prodding gently. Zach hands her the ice pack, and she thanks him. She's grateful to see that the injury is superficial — a scuffed elbow, but no blood. Thank goodness for long-sleeved shirts. Toby now looks calm enough to speak. "Toby," she said, applying the ice, "Please tell Zach how you feel about this." Toby begins crying again, looking daggers at Zach, and says "I don't like it that you pushed me off the swing. My arm really hurts. That was mean! I don't want to play with you anymore!"

"Thanks, Toby. Now Zach knows exactly how you feel about this situation. Zach, do you want to see if there's something you can do for Toby?" Looking down at his shoes, Zach asks Toby if there is anything he needs. Toby asks him for a glass of water and some tissue. Zach goes and gets them. He starts to leave the room and Masako stops him, saying forcefully, "Zach, I'm angry because you broke a very important rule. I want you to take a few minutes to think about why we have that rule about pushing and hitting. Will you please do that? And let me know when you're ready to talk about it with me."

About five minutes later, Zach reappears. Toby is nearby, drawing. "I shouldn't have pushed Toby off the swing," Zach begins. "He hurt his arm."

"That's right," his mom agrees. "We have that rule to keep everybody safe. In this case, we were lucky because Toby's injury isn't too awful. But it could easily have been a lot more serious. That's why I was so angry with you. I'm glad you understand the rule. Zach, what should you do when you get so mad at Toby that you feel like hurting him?"

Zach responds, "Use my words."

"That's right," answers Masako. "It will take a lot of self-control, but I expect you to try really hard next time you get that mad. Words are powerful, and you can let your brother know how angry you are without hurting his body. And," she stands up, brightening, "Now, I'm going to make us a snack, and we'll sit down and discuss the fight you two were having before Toby got pushed." While she's preparing the snack, Masako makes a conscious effort to switch gears, readying herself to take a neutral stance. She then sits the boys down to mediate.

Masako: OK, so both of you are going to talk, and you're both going to listen to each other. I'm going to try and stay in the middle, not taking sides. We're going to be respectful, not call each other names or yell. Understood? (Both boys nod.) Zach,

I'm guessing you were pretty angry at Toby when you pushed him. What was going on?

Zach: We were on the swings. Toby kept saying, (taunting voice) "I can pump higher than you! See how high I can pump?"

Masako: How did that make you feel?

Zach: Um ...

Masako: Were you embarrassed?

Zach: Yeah, it was like when he calls me a baby.

Masako: So, Toby, what was going on for Zach?

Toby: Uh ... I was saying I could pump higher and he ... got embarrassed.

Masako: Thank you ... Zach, did that feeling turn into something different?

Zach: Huh?

Masako: Was there another feeling after you were feeling embarrassed?

Zach: Yeah, I got really *mad* ...

Toby: (Somewhat triumphantly) You got so mad you broke a rule! You hurt me! Besides, you were teasing too!

Masako: (Earnestly, emphatically) Yeah, people sometimes get so furious they lose their self-control ... Toby, what kind of teasing? Can you talk a little bit about that?

Toby: *Before* the swings. We were looking for roly-poly bugs and putting them in plastic cups. Then Zach started bragging about how he had more bugs than me. (He begins to parody his younger brother's loud boasting.) "I have six bugs, and you only have four. I have two more than you! I won! I have two more than you —"

Zach: I wasn't that loud, and I wasn't that mean!

Masako: Perhaps not. I think what's important here is how it made him feel. Toby, can you talk about how the bragging made you feel?

Toby: Embarrassed (long pause.) And then really mad!

Masako: Zach, can you repeat what was happening for Toby?

Zach: I was talking about the bugs —

Toby: — Not just talking! You were *bragging* about the bugs!

Zach: OK, bragging about the bugs ... and Toby got embarrassed that he didn't have as many bugs as I did and then he got mad. That's when he left the garden and went over to the swings.

Masako: (After letting this sink in) I just noticed something interesting. Did you guys notice it too?

Zach: It's kind of the same ...

Toby: Bragging about the bugs and bragging about the pumping ...

Masako: It kind of ... creates the same feelings, doesn't it?

Toby: Yeah ... embarrassed and mad.

Masako: What could you guys do about that?

Toby: No bragging!

Masako: Wow, a "no bragging" agreement? That's huge. Could you really do it? Never brag?

Toby: Maybe ...

Zach: Yeah, but what if you brag, and then I'm still not supposed to? That wouldn't be fair!

Masako: We can talk more about how to resolve this, and I want to hear more ideas from both of you, but I just want to point something out. I think maybe part of what we're talking about here is *retaliation*. Do you guys know what retaliation means? (Blank looks.) It means "getting back" for something you didn't like. I'm wondering if maybe teasing and bragging about the pumping was Toby's way of *retaliating* for Zach's teasing and bragging about the bugs. And then finally Zach *retaliated* for Toby's bragging about the pumping by pushing him off the swing. So things got even worse! Did the problem get solved? (No one answers this, but she has their attention.) Did it end well for either of you? (Both boys look glum.) Just something to think about ... OK, so let's get some more suggestions. Zach, you didn't sound happy with the No Bragging idea. What do you think might work?

Zach: Maybe we shouldn't play together with roly-polies.

Toby: And never go on the swings at the same time? That's silly.

Masako: Toby, we agreed at the beginning to be respectful.

We're just brainstorming here. Let's try to get a lot of ideas out there. Afterward, if you want to criticize an idea, that will be fine. I know you guys can find a way to criticize another person's idea without putting that person down. So, Toby ... was your idea about not swinging at the same time a suggestion, or were you just making a point?

Toby: I don't think never swinging at the same time is a good idea. I was just messing around.

Masako: OK, so do either of you have any more ideas to put out there? (A long pause.) No? OK, we have two suggestions. One is that you guys don't play roly-poly bugs together. The other is that you don't brag. Hmmm ... Zach, what was your worry about the no bragging idea?

Zach: If we have that rule and he brags, what am I supposed to do?

Masako: It sounds like you don't think it would be OK to retaliate, but that leaves you with nothing.

Zach: Kind of ...

Masako: Toby, this is a good time for you to criticize the "don't play with roly-polies" idea, if you have anything to say ... (eyebrows raised, smiling) *respectfully* ...

Toby: Well, what I don't like about that idea is ... sometimes it's fun to play together in the dirt and find bugs.

Masako: Let's think about what's fun about that ...

Toby: It's fun if there's no bragging.

Masako: Interesting.

Zach: How 'bout we play with roly-polies with no bragging?

Masako: Wow, you kind of ... stuck the two ideas together! Toby, would you go for that?

Toby: Yeah.

Masako: That sounds like an agreement. Know what I think? I think this is going to take a lot of self-control. Do you want to try it for a week and then meet again and talk about how it's going? (The boys mumble their assent and begin to fidget. Clearly, they are eager to get the show on the road. Masako pauses: a concern is nagging at her.) Before you go back outside, let's talk a little about what's bragging and what's not bragging, just so we're clear.

Toby: (Sighing; what part of "bragging" does Mom not *get*?) Like (taunting voice) "I have more bugs than you — haha!"

Masako: I see ... but what about if Zach finds a really big roly-poly or ... let's say a funny-looking snail ... and he gets really excited and he says "Oh wow, look at this big dude I found!"? Is that bragging?

Toby (Thinks it over): Not really ...

Masako: Zach, what do you think?

Zach: That's not really bragging ...

Masako: What's the difference? (More fidgeting.) No, really, I'm curious.

Toby: 'Cuz it's not like saying I'm better than you ...

Masako: There's no *comparing* ...

Toby: Right.

Masako: So can we say bragging is more than just being excited and happy that something good happens? Bragging is like saying "I'm better than you"?

Toby: Yeah.

Masako: Zach, does that work for you too?

Zach: Yeah!

Masako: Good. Thanks, you guys. (Turning to face the back door, yelling) Watch out, all your roly-polies! Here they come! (The boys head outside like they've been shot from a cannon.)

### COMPOUND FRACTURE MEDIATION DECONSTRUCTED

Handling a "compound fracture" (a dispute between two kids that results in a violation of house rules) requires you to wear two different hats. With each hat comes a different demeanor and set of behaviors.

Masako wears her "disciplinarian" hat with grace and clarity. For her, discipline is not about shaming or punishing the wrongdoer but rather about teaching him. (After all, the word "disciple" means *learner* or *follower*.) The ritual she employs when one of her boys "loses it" and hurts his brother is working, because physical acting-out is becoming pretty rare at their house. From the get-go, she deployed the wrongdoer to begin making amends — getting the icepack, asking his brother if he needs anything. This little ceremony of restitution began the process of clearing the air. Even if Zach wasn't feeling remorseful, the ritual served as a way for him to at least acknowledge responsibility. If he did feel sorry, it allowed him to act on some of the bad feelings inside. And it made Toby feel less like Zach's victim. Another strategy Masako used to help restore Toby's composure was inviting him to discharge his indignation and anger directly at Zach: "I don't like it that you pushed me off the swing. My arm really hurts. That was mean! I don't want to play with you anymore!" Directly and succinctly, Toby reminded Zach how antisocial behavior makes others feel. It's surprising how much impact this can have. Getting one child to speak directly, even passionately, to another child about out-of-bounds behavior can carry more weight than a dozen parental scoldings.

During this whole process, Masako was stern and businesslike. She was justifiably upset that Zach pushed his big brother, and she let it show. It was clear from her tone that she was serious and feeling provoked, but she was not out of control. She emphasized the "why" of her rule about hurting, allowing Zach time to reinvent and restate the rule and the reason behind it: "I shouldn't have pushed Toby off the swing ... he hurt his arm." She summarized with, "We have that rule to keep everybody safe." Then she validated Zach for knowing that hitting is wrong. Before closing, she walked him through an imagined future event. Here she was putting solid neuroscience to work. By talking through an expectation that Zach "use his words" next time, she helped him set an intention. This builds a pathway in his brain for an alternative behavior to use when he experiences anger in the future, increasing the odds that he will be able to keep on that path.

And much to her credit, Masako isn't a sulker; when it's over, it's over. In order to switch hats, Masako used the time it took to prepare the snack to change gears and re-orient herself. She knew she couldn't mediate if she was still feeling lopsided in her loyalties. (This is a good time for a quick personal emotional inventory — if you're still feeling angry at the offender and sorry for the victim, it might be a good idea to postpone the mediation until those feelings have subsided.) From here on, her challenge was to maintain a neutral demeanor, to be warmly empathetic to both kids, and to ask open, curious questions.

Managing a compound fracture is a balancing act. A few minutes ago, as disciplinarian, Masako was indignant and upset at Zach's behavior — but then as mediator she found herself *explaining* that behavior to Toby: "Yeah, people sometimes get so furious they lose their self-control." She was skating on thin ice here. She was careful to steer clear of justifying what Zach did or holding Toby responsible, which would be blaming the victim. But she did want to cut through some of Toby's self-righteousness. She wanted Toby to understand his role in getting hurt. Her message was that aggression is a predictable human behavior; if you tease or needle someone, you do so at your own risk.

It's not unusual for kids to feel self-righteous, even if they have behaved provocatively, when an exasperated sibling finally hauls off and pops them one. Once kids see that there is a disciplinary consequence after a sibling hurts them, they sometimes develop the mistaken impression that they get an endless pass on obnoxious, provoking behavior. I don't feel parents should ever condone physical retaliation, but at the same time kids need to accept the reality that everyone has a boiling point. Although in the case at hand it's the younger brother who has injured the older one, typically it's younger siblings who become habitual victims, goading older siblings into behavior that demands adult intervention in the form of a consequence. In order for this dynamic not to take root, we have to help the child that was harmed grasp that provocation *is* aggressive — and that it's also risky. Masako delivered her message without belaboring the point: *People sometimes get so furious they lose their self-control.* What worked here was her matter-of-fact tone, as contrasted with the angry voice she had used in chastising Zach. This is about explaining cause and effect, not delivering justice. Kids can hear the difference.

In a couple of instances that followed, Masako took the opportunity for some conflict education. She interrupted the mediation to explore with them the theme of retaliation. Though she knew this might be a little over their heads, she wanted to plant a seed of understanding that "getting back" tends to escalate in a hopeless spiral; it's a "solution" that is in reality a non-solution. This is the kind of parental insight which, when delivered right on the heels of a violent outburst, sounds like a lecture — and usually falls on deaf ears.

Lectures rarely sink in, especially when feelings are high. Masako first took care to help Toby and Zach see how the feelings elicited by bragging — humiliation and anger — were mirrored in both of them. This acted as a softener, making the boys feel more relaxed and open. But she waited until they had surfaced the theme of "getting back" themselves. Then she gave it a name: retaliation. Finally, she shared her thoughts about the futility of endless retaliation. That way, what she had to say sounded more like she was reflecting upon the boys' insights rather than just delivering a canned infomercial.

At the outset of the mediation, Masako found herself wondering how on earth playing with bugs could lead to mayhem, but she started at the end and worked backwards rather than asking how it started. She knows from experience that the boys would probably have very different ideas about who fired the first shot. (See Chapter Six, "Peel the Onion.") Asking Zach to speak first was a way of signaling to both boys that she was feeling neutral and that the disciplinary portion of the process was truly over.

Masako's biggest challenge in this mediation was the Mulling over and Organizing part. The slight difference in maturity between the two boys was very much in evidence. Zach, being younger, came up with a very concrete solution: don't play with bugs together. His reasoning has merit: if you don't play with bugs together, there won't be any fighting about bugs. Toby, being older, got it that bragging was the global problem, but perhaps his solution was a little grandiose: no bragging — ever. Masako suspected that this wasn't do-able. By helping them hybridize their two ideas and suggesting a week-long trial period, she pared the resolution down in scope as well as time frame. She also wanted to make sure everyone was on the same page about what they meant by "bragging." This was important, because kids naturally like to broadcast their successes —"I got 100% on my spelling test!" or "I didn't have any cavities!" — but they can learn to relish their triumphs without lording it over their siblings. So she pressed the boys in order to get clarity from both of them as to what is bragging and what is not — a working definition, so to speak.

Masako thought the resolution was a pretty good one. Since looking for bugs was something both boys not only enjoyed but enjoyed doing *together*, there would be a lot of buy-in from them to refrain from bragging. They would both be motivated to make it go well. This made it a perfect workshop in which to practice self-control. And if this didn't pan out, there was another meeting already in the works.

Toby and Zach are same-sex siblings who are close in age — what psychologists sometimes refer to as "high conflict siblings." This stands to reason. A fifteen-year-old girl and her eight-year-old brother are just not as likely to have a lot of conflict as are two brothers born a year apart. The teenager and her little brother exist in separate spheres, with very little overlap of interests, possessions, or companions. Seen from an ecological perspective, it's as if one of them is a bird and the other a wolf. Occupying distinctly different niches in the same environment, they aren't poised for competition. But a wolf and a fox are a different story, and Toby and Zach often find themselves enmeshed in wolf-fox struggles for a single, crowded niche. As Masako has learned, mediation is a good way to relieve some of the stress of being high-conflict siblings.

## MEDIATION SCENARIO 9

### " ... And Another Thing"

**A CO-MEDIATION**

It's dinnertime, and Elena (11) has asked her parents to mediate. Just about every day, her brother Joseph (8) dumps his jacket and school stuff on the kitchen table in the precise spot where Elena does her homework. There have been a number of spats about this, and now Elena has reached the end of her rope. Their parents, Sharon and Stan, began by reviewing the ground rules. Now they are ready to begin.

Sharon: So, Elena, you wanted to have a talk with Joseph about something. What's up?

Elena: Well, every day after school, he dumps his junk right where I do my homework!

Stan: How does that make you feel?

Elena: It makes me really, really mad!

Stan: Joseph, what's going on for Elena?

Joseph: (Sighing elaborately) She doesn't like it when I leave my stuff on her end of the table.

Sharon: She *doesn't like it*?

Joseph: Yeah, well, she hates it.

Elena: Yes! I really, really hate it!

Joseph: Well, she does things that bug me ...

Elena: Don't change the subject! This is about your stuff on the table!

Sharon: Well, let's just see, Elena. If Joseph has a complaint, he can air it too ...

Elena: That's so unfair. He's just saying that to ... to ...

Stan: To make things even?

Elena: Yeah.

Sharon: Well, I think we should listen to whatever is on anyone's mind. Joseph, what are you thinking about? What does Elena do that bugs you?

Joseph: She calls me Jojo. (Both parents and Elena stare at him in amazement. The family has called him that for as long as anyone can remember. What's the big deal?)

Stan: And, um, that bugs you?

Joseph: It's a baby name!

Sharon: Elena? What's Joseph saying?

Elena: He doesn't like it when I call him Jojo ...

Sharon: Because ... ?

Elena: ... Because ... it's embarrassing?

Stan: Joseph?

Joseph: (Heatedly) Yes! *So* embarrassing!

Sharon: OK, so we have Joseph leaving stuff on the table and we have Elena calling him Jojo. Anything else?

Elena: Well, I don't like your burping!

Sharon: Joseph, how do you think Elena feels when you burp?

Joseph: (Suppressing a smile) She says it's disgusting!

Sharon: OK, so Elena feels disgusted when you burp. (Taking a deep breath. How much more can they pile on?) So we have the clutter on the table, the "Jojo" thing, and the burping. First, let's brainstorm some solutions on the clutter. What are your ideas?

Elena: Put your stuff somewhere else — anywhere else!

Joseph: Just push it out of the way! Why does it have to be such a big deal?

Elena: It's a big deal to me. Just because it's not a big deal to you doesn't mean it's not a big deal to me! Every day I have to look at your books and your jacket and that stupid muffler —

Joseph: And every day I have to hear Jojo this and Jojo that! You said it when Bryce was over and now everyone in my class knows my stupid baby nickname.

Elena: And I have to listen to your burping.

Stan: Whoa ... um, I think maybe we should put the clutter issue and the burping issue in the Parking Lot for a minute. I'd like to hear more about Bryce and ... um, your nickname. Can you talk a little more about that, Joseph?

Joseph: (Struggling to keep his composure) Well, last weekend when Bryce slept over...at breakfast, Elena called me Jojo. So on Monday, Bryce had to open his big mouth and tell everyone in school that my nickname is "Jojo." (He starts to cry softly.)

Elena: Have the other kids been teasing you about that? (He nods mournfully.) Oh, Joseph ...

Sharon: Elena, did you realize it would turn out like that?

Elena: No way. Of course not! (She turns back to her brother and is moved by his tears.) I wish there was something I could do ...

Joseph: (morosely) There's nothing. It's too late.

Elena: Joseph — (she waits for him to look up) I'm really sorry. I wish the kids weren't so mean.

Joseph: (Now he's sobbing) Yeah ... me too.

Sharon: (After a very long pause, allowing Elena's apology and Joseph's mild acknowledgment to sink in) Uh ... would you like us to call you Joseph when other kids are over? (He nods.) What about when it's just the four of us?

Joseph: Either one ... I don't care.

Stan: Will you let us know if that changes?

Joseph: Yeah ... (after a very long pause, he straightens up, somewhat revived. Stan offers a tissue.)

Sharon: Would it be OK to talk about the stuff on the table and the burping? (Both kids look willing.)

Joseph: I can put my stuff someplace else. (Sharon and Stan both shoot looks at Elena.)

Elena: Um ... that would be great.

Sharon: Like where?

Joseph: (Pondering) Well, I don't need the jacket and muffler until the next day, so I could put those in the closet. I could put my books at the other end of the table.

Stan: Where you do your homework.

Joseph: Yeah.

Stan: Makes sense. (Joseph burps, looks surprised, suppresses a laugh. Elena rolls her eyes but doesn't push it. Sharon is trying not to crack up. Stan is smiling good-naturedly.) So ... burping ... is that a story for another day?

Elena: Fine ...

Sharon: Thanks, you guys, good work.

### Co-Mediation Deconstructed

In this situation, the idea of mediating came up at the dinner table, so it was natural for both parents to mediate. Co-mediation is a time-honored model in community-based conflict resolution programs. It's also used in most school-based peer mediation programs. The two-heads-are-better-than-one approach relieves some of the stress on mediators and allows mediation teams to benefit by pooling talent. For example, one partner may be really good about protocol and keeping things on track, whereas the other excels at getting below the surface — what psychoanalyst Theodor Reik called "listening with the third ear." Co-mediation also provides mirroring and balance when necessary. If the parties are involved in a dispute involving racial or gender issues, having one mediator from one group and another mediator from the other group can help ensure that the process feels fair. Divorce mediations often go better if one mediator is a woman and the other a man; nobody feels underrepresented or ganged-up-on.

Co-mediating is great way for parents to learn and practice the technique together. After a session, they can go over what went well and what skills need honing. Co-mediating is also a great way for a parent who feels comfortable mediating to bring the other parent on board. With practice, co-mediation teams become attuned, getting very good at taking turns asking questions and dividing up the responsibilities of running mediation. Each one learns to read his partner's "I got this" or "help me out here" signals — postures, expressions, and gestures. Each comes to respect and appreciate what the other brings to the table.

At the outset, this mediation looked like it was going to be a very conventional sibling quarrel:

- Party One says, *I don't like it when you do a, b, and c*
- Party Two says, *I don't like it when you do x, y, and z*

Generally speaking, this would have been a cakewalk. When two siblings each bring several grievances to the table, it's usually just a matter of time before they realize they can make some trades: I'll stop *a-ing* if you'll stop *x-ing*. Both Sharon and Stan were expecting a tit-for-tat listing of mild annoyances resulting in a swap. But this turned out to be a different situation entirely.

Both parents missed the intensity of Joseph's feelings on the first couple of passes, even though their son stated that Jojo was a baby name and despite his heated and emphatic, "Yes! *So* embarrassing." But Stan's third ear pricked up a little later, when he heard the pain and humiliation behind "You [Elena] said it [Jojo] when Bryce was over and now everyone in my class knows my stupid baby nickname."

It's interesting to speculate where the mediation would have gone if Stan had ignored this cue. The conversation may have remained superficial, entirely sidestepping Joseph's extreme distress. The family's recognition of Joseph's humiliation and misery, Joseph's realization that Elena hadn't set him up intentionally, and Elena's heartfelt apology were all deeply important steps that truly leave matters like clutter and burping in the dust.

One of the hardest kinds of mediations to manage is one in which a wrong can't be righted. If a child loses his brother's library book, he can probably find a way to take responsibility for replacing it. But in the case of loose lips or gossip — or even unintended humiliation, as in this case — it's impossible to get the toothpaste back in the tube. To quote Joseph, "There's nothing. It's too late." Restitution (making things right) is less concrete and therefore more elusive.

Getting Joseph to talk more about his predicament was a great idea. I want to add here that Stan didn't *make* Joseph cry — he *allowed* Joseph to cry. Stan and Sharon agree that crying isn't shameful; it's just a form of expression. Stan doesn't regret eliciting this expression. He knows that his empathy merely let the floodgates open. One result of Joseph's emotional outpouring was that Elena was genuinely touched. She was suddenly indignant on her brother's behalf: ("Have the other kids been teasing you about that?") Though it was clear that Elena immediately regretted using Joseph's nickname in front of company, Sharon was wise to step in here, asking Elena, "Did you realize it would turn out like that?"

This was good power-balancing, because younger children often can't separate wrongdoing from bad intention. Asking Elena this key question gave her daughter a chance to let Joseph know that the hurt was unintended and to begin searching for a way to make it up to him. This led Elena to apologize to Joseph, but without insisting that she do so.

At this point, Sharon stepped a little out of the mediation to ask Joseph how he wanted to be addressed by the family from this day forward. How his parents address him hadn't actually been on the table, but bringing it up was a gesture of respect which, piggybacking on Elena's apology, helped restore Joseph. They could all see it. This emboldened Sharon to try to move ahead with the more mundane issues of the mediation.

Having been respectfully acknowledged, and with an apology under his belt, Joseph was surprisingly ready to be compliant with Elena's request about leaving his things on the table. Sharon took this one step further, by walking him through a plan for what to do with his belongings when he came home the next day. She was counting on this mental rehearsal — setting an intention of future behavior — to increase the odds of his following through.

# MEDIATION SCENARIO 10

## Under the Table

("This Is Going Nowhere")

It's a rainy day, the third in a row. Clarissa (5½ ) and Gabriella (4) are home from school because Clarissa is getting over a cold, and Gabriella is showing signs of having caught the same virus. Their father, Anthony, is trying to work from home on a laptop he has set up in the kitchen. The girls have taken a bedspread from their room and put it over the dining room table to make a cave. It's not long before Anthony hears heated bickering. He knows the girls are grouchy and tempers are short, so he responds quickly to the raised voices.

Anthony: Hey, ladies, what's going on?

Gabriella: She won't be a baby bear.

Clarissa: I *was*. I *was* a baby bear. I let her feed me and wrap me in a blanket, and then she sang the good night song. Now I'm bored, and I want to do something else.

Anthony: Gabriella, what did Clarissa say?

Gabriella: But I wanted to read her a bedtime story, and then we could be done being bears.

Anthony: I hear you. You both want different things. But my question was, what did Clarissa say?

Gabriella: Um ... (it takes her a while to refocus on her sister) She says we played baby bear, and then she got bored.

Anthony: Clarissa, is that about right? (Clarissa nods.) So Gabriella, what's going on for you?

Gabriella: I want to read her a bedtime story. Then we can do something different ...

Clarissa: (Grouchily) You don't know how to read!

Gabriella: (exasperated and insulted) It's *pretend*!

Anthony: So, Gabriella, you want to read to Clarissa, and she doesn't want to be read to? (Gabriella nods.) How do you feel about that?

Gabriella: Sad. Sad and mad ...

Anthony: And maybe disappointed? You were having such a good time, and now she doesn't want to play baby bear any more. Clarissa, what are you hearing?

Clarissa: I don't want to play baby bear anymore, and she's mad and, um ... sad and disappointed.

Anthony: (To Gabriella) Is that about right?

Gabriella: (Glumly) I guess ... (Anthony notices that both girls seem listless. It's as if the fire has gone out of the fight.)

Anthony: What do you want to do about this? (Clarissa looks out at the rain, and Gabriella fiddles with the ties on her hoodie. Anthony waits a full three minutes to see if either of the girls has a suggestion.) You know what I think? I think maybe it's lunchtime in the bear cave! What do you think bears like to eat more than anything in the world?

Clarissa: Honey!

Gabriella: Honey!

Anthony makes peanut butter and honey sandwiches for the girls. As he works, he keeps an ear cocked toward the "cave" under the dinner table, where things remain pretty quiet. The sandwiches are a big hit. A little while later, he hears some more whiny noises. When he comes into the living room, he notices that what had seemed like an endless drizzle is now a full-out storm. "Would the bears like to come out of the cave and look at the weather?" The girls creep out and spend a few quiet minutes watching the rain with him. They talk about the wind and how it's moving the trees in the front yard. All at once, the lights blink off and back on.

This gives him an idea. "Do you want to pretend the power is out?" The girls, remembering a really fun evening last winter when the neighborhood really did lose power, squeal excitedly as Anthony turns out all the lights one by one. He lights a few candles. As all three of them take in the candlelight surrounded by darkness, the room gradually grows very quiet. After a bit, Anthony suggests it might be rest time for bears. "Would you bears like to have some books and flashlights?" He helps them gather up the props and bring them into the cave. He adds a big comforter and some pillows from his bed. The girls arrange a cozy "nest" and settle in with their books. Eventually, Gabriella falls asleep. Clarissa is drowsy, but she manages to stay awake, reading quietly without bothering her sister.

By the time their mother comes home from work, the bears are busy with crayons and drawing pads that they've brought back into their den.

## "This Is Going Nowhere" Mediation Deconstructed

The truth is, there was really nothing to mediate. Anthony figured this out when, after some opening questions, the conflict simply ran out of steam. However, it didn't hurt that he had begun the discussion as he would have begun mediation. The girls got to get things off their chests and feel heard. It's never a waste of time when kids speak their hearts, listen, and reflect. Perhaps it sank in that dramatic play is only fun as long as both participants are enjoying themselves. Once one child gets bored, it's pretty hard to negotiate about continuing. In any case, Anthony correctly inferred that this mediation didn't have legs, and let it go in favor of another approach. He guessed that what the girls needed was something fun to jump-start (and extend) their play. (Psychologists Jerome Bruner and Lev Vygotsky used the term "scaffolding" to describe adult assistance of this type — expanding a play scenario by asking questions, suggesting new story elements and providing fresh props.) Anthony knows that being sick, cranky, and bored saps kids' natural resourcefulness, so he got creative and provided a little more content. What was needed was in fact not mediation but just plain old rainy-day parenting.

# MEDIATION SCENARIO 11

## The Keys to the Car: Take One and Take Two

### (A Do-Over)

**Take One:** It's Tuesday, and Amira, who is about to turn eighteen, and her sister Ashley, sixteen, both want the car Friday night. Since both girls are extremely social, as well as very involved in school extra-curriculars, they have an arrangement with their parents that has been in play since Amira first learned to drive: on Friday nights, the girls have the use of their mother's car and if their parents have plans, Mom and Dad use Dad's car. For a few months last year, Amira was dating a boy from their church, but that didn't last long. The girls are part of a large swarm of friends who usually meet up on Friday evenings. Since Ashley has been driving, the girls have taken turns. Most of the time, they do things with the swarm on Fridays anyway. When their plans differ, one gives the other a ride. So far this has worked for the family.

But this week things are different. Ashley has mentioned to her sister that she would like to have the car by herself to go to a party. Can Amira get a ride with someone else? Amira doesn't get it. Why can't she just drop Ashley off at the party and pick her up in time to get home by curfew? (The girls both have to be back by 12:30.) Over dinner, Amira asks her parents if they have plans for Friday night. She's hoping that if they don't, each girl could use one of the cars. Their mother, Mandy, says they need to drive Dad's car to the next town over for a work-related gathering on Friday night. Disappointed, the girls renew their bickering over Mandy's car. Dad suggests they mediate. Mandy pops up and starts to clear, saying with a smile, "I call dishes." Dad (Leon) settles in to mediate.

Amira: Daddy, can we just skip the ground rules? We know them by heart by now.

Leon: Sure. What's up?

Ashley: Well, Amira and I have different plans this Friday. I really need the car to myself, just this once!

Amira: "Just this once?" Next year I'll be away at college, and you won't have to share the car at all on Friday nights! You'll have it all to yourself!

Ashley: It's just one time! Why are you being so stubborn and selfish?

Amira: (getting up to leave the table) That tears it! (Throws down her napkin) I'm not going to talk to you if you're just going to sit there and insult me! (She stomps off.)

Ashley: (Avoiding her father's gaze, getting up to leave) Well, that was a bust.

Leon: (Putting a hand on her arm) You *really* want the car on Friday night. (Ashley slumps back in her chair.) So what happened?

Ashley: (Big sigh) I lost my temper and I insulted her, and she walked away.

Leon: And ... you still need something from her?

Ashley: (Trying to shrug this off) And I still need something from her.

Leon: (Gently, after a long pause) How's that working for you?

Ashley (Eyes welling with tears of frustration) Not so good.

Leon: Do you know what you want to do?

Ashley: Well, we still need to talk. I have to figure out a way to get her back in the conversation.

Leon: What do you think it would take?

Ashley: (Another big sigh, getting up to leave the kitchen) I gotta figure that out.

Leon: OK, I'm here if you girls need me.

## MEDIATION (TAKE ONE) DECONSTRUCTED

Mulling things over, Leon thought that perhaps it was a mistake to have dispensed with the ground rules. Going over them at the outset of mediation (even if the parties do know them by heart) can set an intention of respect. It might have helped prevent Ashley from flying off the handle. Then again, Leon mused, ground rules aren't magic — something about this feels very high stakes to Ashley, which may be why she lost her composure so early in the game. Leon was dying to know what was really going on. Was this just the tip of an iceberg? Despite feeling curious and uneasy, Leon didn't try to take charge of the problem or even probe too deeply. Instead, he offered what's called conflict coaching to Ashley after Amira huffed out. He asked open questions, just as he would in mediation, and he refrained from giving advice. This took a lot of restraint on his part. What he did was help Ashley lay the problem out in front of her:

- I needed something from my sister
- I lost my temper and insulted her
- I *still* need something from her
- I feel like I have to get this back on track
- How can I do that?

By coaching instead of advising, Leon telegraphed to Ashley that he believes she has the resources to figure this out. He also preserved his neutrality in case the mediation got a restart. Only time will tell.

**Take Two:** It's Wednesday night, twenty-four hours later. Leon and Mandy are worried. Something's up, and they don't have enough information. It feels like Ashley's hiding something. It turns out that late last night, after she cooled off, Ashley went to Amira's room and apologized for her outburst. Having done so, she tried to restart the conversation about the car for Friday night. Amira, feeling a bit wary after the mediation that blew up, suggested they take it up once again with their Dad tonight after dinner.

Leon: So — ground rules. (With a twinkle) Not going to make that mistake again!

Ashley: (Resigned, a little chagrined) I know, I know. No name-calling!

Leon: (To Amira) What else?

Amira: Effort ... I probably gave up too quickly.

Leon: Anything else?

Ashley: I just want to say ... (long pause) I really want this to work. I need this to work. (Both Leon and Amira stare at her hard, trying to fathom her intensity. What is going on? Leon decides that his best bet is to stick to the TABMOC protocol like glue.)

Leon: So, Ashley, what's going on for you?

Ashley: (Deep breath) I need to have the car Friday night. I want Amira to get a ride with someone else just this once.

Leon: Amira? What's up with Ashley?

Amira: Something about wanting the car all to herself Friday night. I just don't see what the big mystery is.

Leon: Amira, please just stick to what Ashley said.

Amira: OK, so Ashley wants the car Friday night. She really, really wants the car Friday night.

Leon: Thanks. And what's going on for you?

Amira: Well, I don't see why one of us can't drop the other one off wherever she needs to go. We always do that when we have separate plans. I don't even care if *she* drives and drops *me* off. I just don't see what the big deal is.

Leon: You sound confused ... Ashley, what's going on for Amira?

Ashley: She wants to do it the way we always do. She doesn't understand why it's different.

Amira: No, I don't!

Leon: Amira, do you want to ask Ashley? (There follows a very long pause.)

Ashley: (Finally) OK fine. I didn't want this to turn into a big deal, but for some reason it's turned into a big deal anyway. I have a date. (Across the room at the sink, her mom turns off the water and stops to stare. The room is eerily quiet.) See what I mean? You guys make such a big deal out of everything! I just didn't want it to be a big deal!

Mandy: (Walking in, quietly) Sweetie, a date ... that's so nice.

Amira: (Talking at the same time as her mother) Who with?

Ashley: (Exasperated) You *guys*!

Leon: OK, ladies, let's calm down. So, Ashley, you have a date.

Ashley: With Jordie Patterson. (Toward her sister) *Since you asked.*

Amira: But Jordie has a car!

Mandy: (To Amira, somewhat relieved) You know him? (Ashley rolls her eyes.)

Amira: Yeah, he's a good friend of Mason's. (Both parents relax, visibly.)

Ashley: (Turning to Amira) I *know* he has a car. When he asked me out, I offered to drive.

Amira: Why?

Ashley: I don't know ... I just kind of blurted it out. We're supposed to go to a party at his cousin's. I don't know the cousin ... I don't know who he hangs out with or what kind of parties they have.

Amira: (Slyly) So the car is your escape plan?

Ashley: You make it sound like some big international spy movie.

Amira: No really, I get it. You don't know Jordie very well yet. If the party goes sideways and Jordie doesn't want to take you home, you're stuck. But if you have the car, you can leave whenever you like, and *he* can get a ride home.

Ashley: If worse comes to worse ...

Amira: Makes sense to me. I'll see if Alicia can take me to Jenny's.

Ashley: Great — thanks!

Leon: Um ... so ... we're done? (The girls murmur their assent and disappear to tackle their homework.)

Mandy: Wow.

Leon: Wow, indeed.

### MEDIATION (TAKE TWO) DECONSTRUCTED

After this mediation, both Leon and Mandy were reeling with all the new information. Leon was rewarded for sticking close to the protocol and waiting patiently for the iceberg to be revealed. At the beginning, he stopped Amira right in her tracks when she was supposed to be acknowledging what Ashley said but was editorializing instead (" ... Something about wanting the car all to herself Friday night. I just don't see what the big mystery is.") Her reframe of this was much more respectful and uncluttered: "Ashley wants the car Friday night. She really, really wants the car Friday night." He took Amira's "I just don't see what the big deal is" back to

Amira, asking if she had a question for Ashley. (Why not let Amira take responsibility for the question that was on everybody's mind?) He let that hang in the air for a bit, and finally Ashley took the cue and told her story. Parents of teenagers know that patience and good timing often make way for better communication than grilling kids for desired information.

Both parents were surprised by the outcome, and yet not surprised. Whereas Amira has always been an open book, Ashley tends to keep things to herself. She has never enjoyed taking center stage or being fussed over, which is why it was hard for her to break the fun news about a first date to her family. Well, maybe Ashley learned something tonight. By being so private and mysterious, perhaps she made things more complicated than they needed to be. After all, once Amira got it, she gave in with sudden willingness: "Makes sense to me. I'll see if Alicia can take me to Jenny's." Amira had been upset because of feeling sidelined, out of the loop. For her, it had never really been about the car.

Finally, things fell into place for Leon and Mandy. And there was another takeaway. They had reason to be grateful that, despite being private and a little inscrutable at times, Ashley is not sneaky, and certainly not reckless. In fact, she's really quite cautious, as demonstrated by her wish to take the wheel Friday night.

# MEDIATION SCENARIO 12

## The Building Blocks of Conflict Resolution

It's a Sunday afternoon in July. Carter is hoping his kids Seth (7) and Tessa (5) will play peacefully together. He would love to spend some time in the hammock with the Sunday paper before his wife gets back with the groceries, which he has promised to transform into a barbeque dinner. So he has reason to be dismayed when he hears the kids' building set — an enormous collection of wooden blocks — spill out on the kitchen floor. It's been months since Seth and Tessa have been able to play peacefully with the blocks. His repeated suggestion that they take turns, since they can't seem to play nicely together, falls on deaf ears. Again and again, they return to the scene of discord, and the whole unpleasant business begins afresh.

He was right to be worried. The yelling begins just as he has balanced his lemonade on a tree stump and settled into the hammock. His kids seem almost magnetically drawn to this particular conflict situation. Why they haven't figured out a way to avoid this dispute is quite beyond him. Curiosity and exasperation compete for his attention. Finally, curiosity wins. He picks up his lemonade and walks back into the house. He marches into the kitchen and announces that he's going to mediate with them. He goes over the ground rules as he pours them each a glass of lemonade and tosses a fistful of ice in each glass.

Carter: OK, guys, this thing with the blocks has been happening over and over again. I don't understand it very well, but something's not working. So, let's sit over here and talk it through. We're going to use our indoor voices and show respect. No insults or put-downs, OK? (They nod glumly.) I'm going to try to stay in the middle and not take sides. So what seems to be going on?

Tessa: Seth is always grabbing!

Seth: Yeah, well you're always being bossy and yelling!

Carter: OK, Tessa. The grabbing. How does that make you feel?

Tessa: Sad ...

Carter: Can you tell Seth that?

Tessa: Seth, it makes me sad ...

Carter: "When you ... "

Tessa: When you ... grab the blocks.

Carter: Thanks, Tessa. Seth, did you hear what she said? Can you say it for us?

Seth: (Impatiently) I *heard* what she said. But what about the yelling?

Carter: We'll get to that, I promise. But first we need to be sure that you heard Tessa. Can you say it for us?

Seth: (Resigned) She gets sad when I grab the blocks.

Tessa: (Hotly) Yeah!

Carter: OK, good work, guys. Now Seth, what's going on for you?

Seth: She's so bossy!

Carter: Well, Seth, you and Tessa agreed to talk respectfully, and calling her a name isn't respectful. Can you say that another way? (Seth is looking very grumpy.) Talk about the *behavior* you don't like.

Seth: Um, the yelling and ... ordering me around.

Carter: Sounds like you get annoyed when she yells ... and gives orders. Tessa, can you let Seth know you heard him?

Tessa: (To Seth) You get annoyed when I yell. And when I try to be the boss. But Daddy —

Carter: Hang on, Tessa. Seth, is that about right?

Seth: (Sighing elaborately) Yes.

Carter: Thank you both. OK, so what do you think can be done? We're going to throw out a bunch of ideas at first, as many as you can think of. For right now let's not criticize or discuss the suggestions, just collect them.

Seth: I think we should play with no yelling.

Tessa: I think we should play with no *grabbing*!

Carter: OK, we have two ideas. Any others? (The kids just

glower at each other. There is a very long pause.) Um, just to move things along here — what do you guys like about playing with the blocks? Seth?

Seth: Uh ... it's fun. I like to concentrate.

Carter: (Warming, relieved that someone is talking) Concentrate how?

Seth: I like to build really tall towers. It's hard. You have to concentrate really hard.

Carter: You get a lot of satisfaction from building tall towers. It's really pleasant for you to *focus*.

Seth: (A bit dreamily) Yeah.

Carter: Tessa? What do you like about playing with the blocks?

Tessa: I like to make things.

Carter: Like what kind of things?

Tessa: Things ... that you can put stuff in. Um, like a house ... or a barn.

Carter: I've noticed that. You know something else I've noticed? I never thought about this before, but Seth spends almost all his time on the *building* part. Tessa, you tend to build something quickly and then spend most of your time making up stories or games that go on inside it. You both use the blocks in your own way. And the two ways are really different. (Long pause.) Any other ideas of how to play peacefully with the blocks?

Seth: (To his dad) *You* always say, why don't we take turns?

Carter: You mean not use the blocks at the same time? Do you want to put that down as a suggestion?

Seth: (Without much enthusiasm) We could ... (a glance at Tessa tells Carter that she is uninspired.)

Carter: So we have three ideas: no grabbing, no yelling, take turns. (Long pause) Well, let me ask you this: what do you like about playing *together* with the blocks? No, really — I'm itching to know, because to me it looks like playing together often ends in a fight. And yet you don't seem very excited about the idea of playing separately. So I'm really confused and, uh, sort of curious.

Tessa: (Quietly) Seth is a good builder.

Carter: Talk about that a little bit.

Tessa: Um, he builds tall things. Sometimes when I try to build tall things, they fall down.

Seth: Well, I'm *seven*.

Carter: I think you're both being very generous. Tessa, you complimented Seth, and Seth, your response was sort of interesting. It sounds like you're saying that as Tessa gets older, she'll learn to be a better builder too. Is that right?

Seth: Yeah, I guess.

Carter: What will it take for her to become more skillful?

Seth: Huh?

Carter: Um, will Tessa become a better builder by just waiting for seven candles on her birthday cake?

Seth: (Chuckling) No ... she's gotta practice. (Turning to Tessa) You gotta *practice*.

Carter: This is a big guess I'm making ... but Seth, I bet it's hard to be patient and watch someone try and have the blocks fall, and try and have the blocks fall *again*. Does that make you feel like grabbing?

Seth: I guess so ...

Carter: It takes patience to keep your hands in your pockets and watch someone practice so they get good at it too! (Long pause while he lets this sink in.) For now, let's put grabbing and yelling in the Parking Lot, 'cause right now I want to turn the same question around. Seth, why do you like to play blocks with Tessa?

Seth: It's fun ... sometimes.

Carter: (Smiling) It's fun when there's no yelling, right? Fun in what way?

Seth: She puts in the people ... or, um ... the animals and then ... stuff happens.

Carter: Sounds like she's good at providing characters and a plot.

Seth: Yeah.

Tessa: (Liking where this is headed, but a little perplexed by the language) Huh?

Carter: I think Seth likes the people and the animals you bring into the building, and the stories you make up. Is that right? (Seth nods.)

Seth: I have an idea — how 'bout I make the building and then when I'm done Tessa can put in the characters, and we can play with them together? (Tessa starts to look distressed.)

Carter: Tessa, I can see you're not crazy about that idea, but right now we're just collecting suggestions. So far we have no yelling, no grabbing, play separately, and play in two stages with Seth designing and building and then both of you playing together with Tessa's characters and story. Wow, this is getting complicated! Any other ideas?

Tessa: I wanna help do all that stuff too!

Carter: You mean the designing and the building? (She nods emphatically.)

Seth: (Disappointed, beginning to lose heart) Oh man ...

Carter: Seth, it's not time to criticize yet. We have a whole bunch of ideas on the table. I'm going to write them down. I'll make pictures, so it's real clear. He gets a huge piece of butcher paper and writes down all the ideas with stick-figure pictures next to each one:

- No yelling (open-mouthed face with a line through it)
- No grabbing (outstretched hand with a line through it)
- Play separately (two kids, each with a pile of blocks, sitting apart)
- Seth plans and builds, and then you play together using Tessa's story and characters (girl stands and watches the boy build, then they sit and play together at the structure — girl's mouth is open)

- Both kids plan and build, then they play together using Tessa's story and characters (both kids building, mouths open, then both kids playing — girl's mouth open)

Seth: I have another idea. If we're both going to design and build, then I want to help with the story and the people. (Tessa looks crestfallen.) Well, it's more fair!

Carter: OK, I'm adding that suggestion to the list. (By now both kids look a little overwhelmed.) Boy, this is hard work. But you guys are doing great! You've come up with so many different options. Anybody need a pit stop? (They decide to take a five-minute break. Carter scribbles idea six on the butcher paper and adds a quick sketch. Then he and Tessa each go to the bathroom. Seth runs outside to check on the dog and refresh his water bowl. Carter refills the glasses with lemonade. All the while he's thinking about the yelling and grabbing and wondering how and when to fit them into the conversation. Everyone comes back in and sits down.) So before we go over all the suggestions, I want us to talk a little bit about the yelling and the grabbing. Seth, it sounds like you sometimes grab when you're feeling impatient with Tessa's building process. Is that right?

Seth: Yeah.

Carter: And does the yelling happen after you grab?

Seth: Yeah, but not *just* when I grab. She yells when she's trying to be the boss, like "Do it this way. No, do it that way!" I don't like being bossed around!

Tessa: But you never build what I want!

Carter: Wow, Tessa, "never" is such a strong word. Can you say that another way? "I feel ... "

Tessa: I feel ...

Carter: Feel what? Angry? (Pause) Frustrated? (Long pause) Disappointed?

Tessa: I feel mostly ... sad ... when ... you don't build what I say. (Long pause.)

Carter: What you've said gets me thinking ... having Seth do all the building is sort of a shortcut!

Seth: Huh?

Carter: Well, if she's having trouble building, oh let's say, a silo for the farm, and you grab the blocks and take over, the silo gets built faster. And if she can get you to build what she says, by ordering you around, she gets the building she wants without having to build it! That's what I mean by "shortcut." But then she doesn't get the practice she needs that you talked about before. Does that make sense? (Seth nods, but Carter can see that he's losing Tessa. He goes back to the butcher paper.) OK, let's see what we have so far:

- No yelling (open-mouthed face with a line through it)
- No grabbing (outstretched hand with a line through it)
- Play separately (two kids, each with a pile of blocks, sitting apart)
- Seth plans and builds and then you play together using Tessa's story and characters (girl stands and watches the boy build, then they sit and play together at the structure — girl's mouth is open)
- Both kids plan and build, then they play together using Tessa's story and characters (both kids building, mouths open, then both kids playing — girl's mouth open)
- Both kids plan and build, then play together using a story and characters they make up together (both kids building,

mouths open, then both kids playing — both kids' mouths open)

Carter: So what do you think?

Tessa: I like no yelling and no grabbing.

Carter: Seth?

Seth: Yeah, me too.

Carter: Wow, that was easy! But it's gonna take a lot of self-control, isn't it? (He pauses for a few beats to let this sink in.) What about "play separately?" (Both kids make a face.) Yeah, that was a "dad idea." I never did get anywhere with that one (Seth squirms, Tessa giggles. Carter crosses it out.) OK, so what about idea four — where Seth plans and builds and then you play Tessa's story?

Seth: Wait! What if I want to build an airport, and she wants to play farm?

Tessa: That would be silly. It wouldn't work

Carter: Should I cross that idea out? (They nod.) So what about number five — you both plan and build and then play together using Tessa's ideas?

Seth: I like the last one the best.

Carter: Number six?

Seth: Yeah. We both plan and build, and then we both do the story and the characters. It's the most fair.

Carter: (Thoughtfully) Huh. I want to add something to that ...

earlier, I heard you both say admiring things about each other ... about the way you play. Tessa said Seth builds tall towers. It sounded like she wants to learn how. And Seth said Tessa is good with plots and characters, but he wants practice with that too ...

Tessa: It *is* the most fair ... it's the best one.

Carter: OK, so I've crossed out ideas three, four, and five. But I just want to say that number six might be the hardest one of all to do. I sure think the No Yelling and the No Grabbing will help. But it's going to be a challenge. Think you can do it? (They are clearly restless and eager to get to work on a project.) Tell you what, why don't you give it a try right now. But let's plan to get back together tomorrow night after dinner and talk about how it went, OK? (The kids mumble their assent and begin gathering the blocks together.) I'll post these three rules on the wall nearby, so you can see them. Thanks, you guys. You really put in a lot of effort on this. I hope it pays off!

## THE BUILDING BLOCKS OF CONFLICT RESOLUTION MEDIATION DECONSTRUCTED

It was a good idea for Carter to begin by stating his bafflement to the kids. It was curiosity, after all, that drove his desire to mediate. Despite going over the ground rules, he found that he had to insist on reframes more than once ("She's so bossy" ... "he always ... ")

There was a lot of power-balancing to be done. His aside to Seth about "character" and "plot" had to be dialed down for Tessa: "... the people and the animals you bring into the building, and the stories you make up." Twice, Carter coached Tessa when it was her turn to talk about her feelings: "Seth, it makes me sad when you grab the blocks;" "I feel ... sad ... when you don't build what I say." He also provided the word "annoyed" so that she could accurately reflect what Seth felt about her yelling. Writing everything down and drawing pictures to illustrate the kids' suggestions was a great way to keep track of some pretty complex ideas while making the list accessible to both children — one who can read and one who cannot.

Carter took the mediation beyond the "no grabbing/no yelling" phase by switching focus from the children's positions to their interests: what do they like about playing with the blocks? Both kids were quite forthcoming, and this allowed Carter to spotlight the distinct difference in their play styles. This is where being a keen observer of his kids really paid off. He was right on the money with his description of the unique way each of them plays with blocks. Then he took it a step further by asking what they like about playing *together*. This prompted a compliment from Tessa: "Seth is a good builder." What followed was an interesting side trip about how kids become skillful. Carter used a delicate touch here. He may have been thinking, *How the heck is your little sister going to learn to build a tower if you keep grabbing?* but instead he let Seth "invent" the idea that Tessa needs practice. He offered Seth empathy instead of criticism: "I bet it's hard to be patient and watch someone try and have the blocks fall, and try and have the blocks fall *again*. Does that sometimes lead to grabbing?" Not only did this validate Seth's frustration, but it may have offered some insight to Tessa about what provokes grabbing.

At this point, Carter was looking at a fork in the road. The connection between the yelling and the grabbing was certainly interesting, but he also wanted to provide the symmetry of asking Seth why it was fun to play blocks with Tessa. This turned out to be a great choice because Seth had some kind things to say about his sister's gift for dramatic play. Not only did this provide a "softening" compliment to balance Tessa's, but it also led them to add more suggestions to the list.

The break was well-timed. It gave the kids a chance to work off some of their restlessness, and it provided Carter with time to ponder how to handle a pretty ungainly list of options. It occurred to him number one and two were about *behavior* and numbers three through six were about *process*. He decided to return to grabbing and yelling before comparing the final four (process) options. Here Carter put in his two cents with the idea that having Seth do all the building was a shortcut, but he didn't belabor the point when he saw that this was over Tessa's head. Recapping the very first part of the mediation (letting both kids restate how the grabbing and yelling made them feel) softened their approach and prompted them to agree to the first two suggestions without debate. Carter let go of number three (the "dad idea") with humor and good grace. Suggestions numbers four, five, and six turned out to be variations on the same theme, each one more inclusive and fair than the one before it. This was plain as day to the two children.

As it happened, even after the mediation, Seth and Tessa still found it challenging to play with the blocks together. What they had accomplished that afternoon was to come up with some guiding principles about how they were going to play. That's huge, but it wasn't enough. Principle is one thing, and application is another. The next night, Carter made good on his suggestion that they meet again. During this second mediation, the kids identified specific challenges. Then they came up with some ideas about how they could talk and plan before laying the first block.

None of this would have worked if there had not been a lot of will to play *together*. (It's easy to see how another pair of siblings, frustrated with the difficulty of "playing nicely together" with the blocks, might wisely decide to play separately.) All Carter knew at the outset of the mediation was that both kids preferred playing with blocks together, despite all the yelling and grabbing, than they did playing alone with them. Clearly, they were seeking a level of collaboration that was out of reach. Though meeting twice took a lot of time and effort, it enabled the kids to attain some of the synergy they had been striving for.

# 4

# HELPFUL QUESTIONS

*I*t should be clear from the scenarios in Chapter Three that good questions are the very heart of mediation. I like to think that when we ask our children good questions, we are educating them in the highest and purest sense; after all, the Latin word *educare* means "to draw out from." Try to ask questions that are probing and curious. The key is to be inquisitive without being inquisitional. When people get the scent of accusation or distrust, they shut down. Obviously, a self-protective stance is not conducive to open communication. You are questioning for understanding, not to catch someone or corner him. Staying neutral is your touchstone when you mediate. The tone of your questions will protect — or undermine — the process.

The goal is to get your children sharing information. You'll find that questions with a "yes or no" answer don't yield much material. Try to frame questions that are wide enough to drive a truck through! It's okay if you don't know what the answer will be — in fact, it's even better if you can't imagine where things are going. That means the parties can determine the direction of the mediation themselves. You are only there to maintain the flow and keep the tone respectful. You do this in part by keeping the questions coming

— questions that are curious, imaginative, empathetic, and non-judgmental. A good mediator models openness of heart and mind.

Always wonder about the feeling *under* the feeling, or the feeling *before* the feeling. Siblings are used to having their brothers and sisters mad at them. "Mad" might be so commonplace that it's a little boring. For example, it's enlightening for Henry to learn that before his sister Luisa got mad at him she was frightened (or disgusted or saddened, for example) by what he did. The final emotion that she has presented to him (mad) can be traced back to something else that is actually quite different, and this knowledge might be useful to Henry in reflecting upon his behavior.

Keep the good questions coming. Following are some ideas about framing open-ended questions.

**Some questions, in no particular order, which meet the "wide enough" criterion:**

- What's going on?
- What do you think happened?
- How did you feel about that?
- How did that affect your feelings?
- How did you feel when [s]he said that?
- Do you remember how you felt when it first happened?
- What would it take for you to feel differently about this?
- What happened right before that?
- How were you feeling right before that?
- Is there something you'd like to bring up that you're maybe a little worried about discussing?
- Could you talk a little more about that?
- What did you want/expect him/her to do?
- What will it look like if this happens again?
- What would it feel like to do it in this new way instead?
- Does this remind you of something else?
- What did you mean when you said _____?
- What's really, really important to you about this?
- What will it feel like for you if we don't solve this?

- What would it take for you to feel like we've solved this?
- Can you say that another way so [s]he might understand you better?
- How did you ... ?
- Why did you ... ?

A mediator asks questions a journalist might ask in order to get information. This opens up a space in which kids can communicate, share feelings, and collaborate. Anything that sounds like an inquisition can cause that space to close up — a missed opportunity, to be sure. But it feels like open questions are quite different from how our parents questioned us — and how we may approach our own kids when behavior goes out of bounds. It's often true that the questions we automatically reach for (in knee-jerk reaction to conflict) are unhelpful. Open questions lead us toward a deeper understanding, not just about the issue at hand, but about our children — who they are and who they hope to be.

# NOT-SO-HELPFUL QUESTIONS

*T*his chapter will be a little longer than the previous one, and for a reason. In order to mediate effectively, there may be a few habits to break!

GOTCHA QUESTIONS

One problem is that the questions we tend to ask children when something has gone wrong are gotcha questions that sound like they come straight out of the justice system. These questions assume an offender and a victim (or a plaintiff and defendant) instead of just two people with a problem to solve. Gotcha questions, such as "What did you do to him?" are legalistic and accusatory. They make the plaintiff feel aggrieved and self-righteous. They make the defendant feel — well, *defensive* and self-righteous. This line of questioning is polarizing, so it arouses feelings that are barriers to mediation. An open-ended, neutral question such as "What happened?" avoids the offender/victim framework and so helps to neutralize conflict. A dispute is, simply, what happens when two people disagree and/or behave disrespectfully toward one another.

· · ·

## Convergent Questions

It's a truism that a lawyer should never ask a witness a question that the lawyer herself doesn't know the answer to. That's because the lawyer must direct all her questions toward an intended conclusion. Lawyers are supposed to ask *convergent questions*, because it's their job to home in on the predetermined target, which of course is the "truth" that they are promoting. Mediators, on the other hand, have no target, so we ask *divergent questions* — wide enough to accommodate that proverbial truck. Here are some examples of convergent questions, the kind that *aren't* helpful in mediation:

- Questions with a yes or no answer (these tend to stop the conversation dead)
- Multiple choice questions (an answer that isn't prompted will usually be more rich, detailed, and accurate)

## Roads to Nowhere

In my experience, these two time-honored questions are a complete waste of time:

- Who started it? (Or its variant: Whose fault is it?)
- Who had it first?

Every child knows the answers to these questions: *The other kid started it, and I had it first!*

When it comes to who started it, kids almost always say it was the other child who made the first move. You may have noticed that grownups in conflict do the same thing. I don't believe that people do this just in order to save face or avoid punishment. People in conflict actually *believe* that the other person initiated the conflict. They feel that their behavior was within bounds and defensible — it was the other person who crossed the line. That's just how things look when we're involved in an escalating dispute. As for who had it first, this is often beside the point. For example, an older sibling may have been hogging the TV remote all morning despite his younger sibling's continued entreaties that he share. What matters here is not that "possession is nine-tenths of the law" (a legalistic solution), but rather how they are going to work out the fact that the household has two kids and one remote (a mediated solution).

## GREAT QUESTIONS, ROTTEN TIMING

There's a class of questions that are really terrific when they are asked at the right time. Unfortunately, we usually ask them at a bad time and in the wrong way — when we come upon the scene of the dispute, and especially if the conflict has become physical. (We read about a Compound Fracture in Chapter Three, Scenario 8; there is more about Compound Fractures at the beginning section of the next chapter.) We've all seen — or been — that angry parent barking questions at a child who we think has committed some misdeed:

- Why did you do that?
- What were you thinking?
- What made you want to do that?
- How would you feel if someone did that to you?

The questions, asked at this time and in this way, are rhetorical. Not really questions at all, they mean something other than what they seem to mean. The *words* of the questions express a curiosity about the dispute, but the *tone* conveys, simply and forcefully, "I am absolutely furious with you!"

There are a couple of reasons not to ask these particular questions when you are really, really mad. The first reason is that kids usually don't realize the questions are rhetorical. To a young child, every question deserves an answer. Not mature enough to come up with a self-reflective answer, and intimidated by your anger, a child will probably answer "because" or "I don't know." If that isn't enough to hurl you around the bend, I can't think what is! You're already mad — let's not make things worse by asking questions that invite crazy-making answers, the kind that only amplify your fury and strain your composure.

The other reason I advise not asking these questions at the outset is that they are actually excellent ones to put on hold and to pose later, in mediation — once the kids (and you, the parent) have calmed down and are really listening to one another. Let's look at them again in this different light. Think what these exact same questions might yield if asked in a curious, calm, openhearted way:

- Why did you do that?
- What were you thinking?
- What made you want to do that?
- How would you feel if someone did that to you?

With practice, you will become accustomed to asking helpful questions and steering clear of unhelpful ones. The next chapter includes a variety of tips and tricks from the mediation toolbox. Hopefully these methods will sustain you and help refine the way you assist your kids with conflict resolution.

## 6

# MEDIATION TECHNIQUES AND HELPFUL HINTS

*C*onflict in and of itself is not misbehavior. Siblings having a dispute are not being naughty; they are working on a problem. Perhaps there is a disagreement, or they want the same toy, or one has hurt the other's feelings. Conflict is commonplace and an altogether normal human engagement. So mediation is never a punishment, and it shouldn't feel like one. In fact, mediation fits into family life much the way real-world mediation fits side-by-side with our legal system. Mediation is a departure from prosecution and fault-finding because it focuses only on problem-solving. Mediation comes into play not when a statute is violated (which would involve the justice system) but when two citizens, or two business entities, have a gripe with one another.

UNDERSTAND THE ROLE OF MEDIATION IN YOUR FAMILY'S GOVERNMENT

Every family is like a tiny government, with its own law of the land. It's your job as parent to uphold the law of the land. After all, you created those rules, and if you don't enforce them, who will? Mediations happen alongside (and distinct from) family discipline.

I should point out here that when I say "discipline," I'm talking about a sprawling and comprehensive system. It's not just about limits and consequences. It's your family's code or mission statement — your values and aspirations. It's the routines, schedules, and standards that govern your daily life. It's about consistency, staying the course. It's about expectations and communication. It encompasses the myriad things a child needs to be taught in order to function as a capable, ethical, and compassionate person in the world. And yes, of course it includes limits and consequences. But I think discipline is every bit as much about parents regulating themselves as it is about parents regulating their children.

I'll illustrate this with an example from daily life. It doesn't work to jump off the couch at 7:55 PM and shriek to your five-year-old, "Oh, look at the clock — you've got to be in bed in five minutes!" (Anyone who has ever spent time with a child will agree with me that this isn't going to end well. Or on time.) You, as the person in charge, need to be mindful of how long the whole bedtime routine takes (bath, brushing teeth, a storybook, whatever matters to you.) Let's say that's forty-five minutes. Factor in a five-minute warning. This means you tell your child at 7:10 that in five minutes it will be time to start getting ready for bed. Then you begin the routine at 7:15, as promised. You will probably have to shadow your child during this whole process until the routine gets ingrained. That's discipline — for both of you. Children find it much easier to behave well when expectations are clear and follow-through is consistent.

Naturally, there have to be consequences when a family rule is broken. But here's where it gets tricky. Often, two siblings are arguing and then somebody gets so excited they break a family rule — for example, "we don't hurt each other." I call this a Compound Fracture because it has two parts: the spat the children are having compounded by the breaking of one of the laws of the land. Let's say Janet and Judy are arguing over a doll, and Janet slaps her younger sister. To ignore that Janet broke a family rule — especially a violation that is painful, dangerous, or insulting — and just go straight to mediation would be like walking through a burning building to turn off the stove. I suggest that first you deploy your justice system for Janet's misbehavior, and then allow the girls to mediate the original conflict that was left unresolved. Once justice has been served, your mediation will probably go more smoothly, because all of you can focus on how they are going to solve the problem with the doll (primary issue) with the hitting episode (secondary incident) settled and out of the way. As a parent you wear a lot of hats, and the trick is remembering which one to put on when, as well as how you want to behave when you're wearing it. (We saw a mom disciplining, then mediating, in Chapter Three, section 8, "Compound Fracture.")

It's very, very common for the initial dispute to get lost in the shuffle after a compound fracture. When one sibling hurts the other, feelings are high. Everyone is distracted by the act itself, as well as the necessary remedies (bandages, a cold pack) and the ensuing emotions — indignation, concern, remorse, and so forth. For the parent, disciplining takes time and energy and patience. But as weary as you may feel after dispensing justice, everybody will probably benefit in the long run if you switch hats and start mediating. The reason is simple: the argument the kids were having still lingers in the air. An unresolved conflict is likely to re-set itself in a fresh (but related) dispute before long. Why not nip it in the bud? Another good reason for going back and mediating the primary issue is that every successful resolution of a conflict will underscore the fundamental truth: there's a better way to settle a dispute than by hurting someone.

### STAY NEUTRAL: MEDIATOR, KNOW THYSELF

This is a memorable piece of advice given to me by Avis Ridley-Thomas, who was director of L.A.'s Dispute Resolution Program when I was training at the DRP to become a mediator. Self-awareness is fundamental to the work we do. Unless I am aware of my own personal needs, limitations and biases, I cannot set them aside in order to be neutral. This is what Avis calls "protecting the integrity of the process." For a parent, knowing when not to mediate is just as important as all the mediation techniques one can master. When there is a shortage of time, patience, or neutrality, other kinds of dispute resolution (e.g., arbitration, postponement, handing the matter off to another adult) are for the best. (More about this in Chapter Seven, "When to Mediate and When to Arbitrate.")

Self-awareness requires some personal excavating and reflection. If you grew up with siblings, take time to think about those relationships. Adults with siblings usually carry the residue of old childhood resentments and alliances. Often, these feelings are rekindled when adults encounter their own kids' rivalries and disputes. If, for example, you were the youngest in your family, you might tend to overreact when your older child lords it over the other(s). Or if you grew up as the older sibling, you could be extra-annoyed by the pestering antics of your younger child. It's worth your while to think about old attachments and grudges that you carry within you, and to try not to let them influence the way you oversee your own children's relationships. This kind of self-reflection is encouraged in a profound and inspiring way in Hartzell and Siegel's *Parenting from the Inside Out*.

Also consider the question, "How am I like my children and how are we unalike?" Similarities and dissimilarities of appearance, intellect, temperament, and aptitude color how we feel about each of our children and how we interact with them. This is not about love. I love both my kids to pieces, but just as I took an irrational measure of joy from his dimple (like mine!) and her love of singing (like me!) it has been vexing to see in them character traits that I see as liabilities or flaws in myself. Coming to terms with these similarities and differences can help steer us away from cutting a child too much slack on the one hand, or being overly harsh on the other. We can only embrace neutrality if we acknowledge bias.

The most vivid and useful description of neutrality I ever heard came from mediator Eric Stephens. Eric is a community-minded citizen who has given of his talents to educate youth about conflict resolution and to involve them in school-based gardening projects. I got to know him through our volunteer work in two wonderful community mediation organizations, Centinela Youth Services and the Western Justice Center. Eric told me, "My client is the space between the two parties."

## DON'T LET THE MEDIATION START WITHOUT YOU

If your children are quite small, you will probably have little trouble using your authority to get them to mediate. With older children, and especially teenagers, what mediators call "convening" (arranging and planning a mediation) could be half the battle. (Marlene faced this challenge in Chapter Three, Section 4.) Sometimes it works better to suggest mediation to each of them separately. This can give you a chance to work through any resistance they may be feeling. The tips that follow are particular to this type of situation.

For mediators, there can be a fine line between convening and the actual mediation itself. When feelings are high, especially anger, it's natural for the parties to begin venting the minute the mediator contacts them. A certain amount of letting off steam before things get under way can be a good thing, if it is met with lots of active listening on the part of the mediator. Being heard ("feeling felt") calms the parties and enables them to focus on what's important to them. This boosts their capacity to be composed and respectful when they sit down to mediate with the conflict partner.

However, from the get-go you must balance your empathetic presence with clear disclaimers about neutrality. Both kids need to know upfront that you are not going to take sides. If your child were to enter into the process believing you are allied with her, only to find that you are not acting as her advocate, she might feel confused or even betrayed.

Convening is also a good time to start talking a little bit about ground rules with each child, especially if mediation is new to your family. Ground rules generally serve to make parties feel safer. You should then go over the ground rules once the kids are sitting together in front of you, and you'll want to get a clear buy-in from both of them in the presence of one another before actually starting. Sometimes it works to have very angry or upset parties *formally* agree to the ground rules while they are still separated. Once you get them together, begin by carefully restating the rules that everyone has already agreed on. This starts the mediation in a positive way, after all, the process has begun on a note of agreement.

There are two things I think you should be especially careful to avoid when you are inviting the kids to mediate: advising and shuttle diplomacy. It's tempting, when you are alone with each of them, to over-coach, sharing tips and ideas for how *you* think it could go well. Hang on tight to the idea that the expressions of feelings as well as the proposed solutions must be *theirs*. It's also tempting to keep them in separate quarters, running back and forth with toned-down versions of what each has to say to the other, along with dressed-up offers and counteroffers. I would only use shuttle diplomacy in extreme cases, as when kids are so agitated they might get physical. Even then, I would only go for a concession or two by shuttle, striving to complete the mediation face-to-face.

Convening sets the tone. It lets the kids know that this will be something different, a ceremony of respect of sorts. Take time to explain things fully and to answer any questions your kids may have. Some skepticism is to be expected! To summarize, when convening, *do*:

- Listen carefully and caringly
- Provide validating feedback (active listening)
- Let them know you plan to take a neutral stance
- Introduce the idea of ground rules

And try to avoid:

- Advising and/or providing tips
- Over-coaching
- Proposing solutions
- Shuttle diplomacy (except in extreme cases)

## HELP THEM UNPACK

To some degree, we all speak in our own private code. The encoding/decoding process sometimes reminds me of a magic suitcase. One person packs the suitcase with certain contents and another person unpacks it, finding very different contents! How can that be? We've all written an email (or said something) that we felt was clear. However, our reader/listener inferred all sorts of things that we didn't intend to convey. Over and over again, we are reminded that communication is imperfect. It isn't unusual for two people to be arguing over a word or phrase only to find out that they each assign a different meaning to the expression, or that they attach opposing emotional reactions to it. When you hear one of your kids say something that might be unclear to the other child or over his/her head, ask the speaker to clarify. Similarly, loaded words or phrases should be broken down. (We saw how Jeff reacted to the word "privacy" in Chapter Three, Section 2.) To identify words or expressions that are likely to need clarification, watch the listener as well as the speaker. You may see signs of disbelief, hurt, bewilderment or shock. Help the speaker make clear the meaning, simplify the message, or expand upon loaded expressions:

- *Can you talk a little more about that?*
- *Could you break that down into smaller parts?*
- *Hmm ... is there another word for that?*
- *What does that word [expression] mean to each of you?*

## RELY ON REFRAMES

Often when siblings are in conflict, they say things that are insulting, presumptuous, or judgmental: "You're so immature!" or "You did that because you want to be the boss of everything." These kinds of remarks aren't exactly packaged for maximum positive impact, but they often hold useful, honest material for discussion. Reframing takes kids back to the ground rule about respect. Renowned mediator Kenneth Cloke says, "reframing is removing the poison while preserving the message." When mediating, you can construct a reframe with some active listening and by encouraging the speaker to use an I-message. (There will be more about active listening and I-messages in Chapter Nine, "Relationship Talk.") Helping with reframes of the above statements might look something like this:

"You're so immature!" This is a label and an insult, so I would begin by referring back to the ground rules. "Henry, to me that doesn't sound respectful ... and you and Mara did agree to talk respectfully to each other. What I'm hearing is that something she did really bothered you (active listening.) Can you tell her what that was and how it made you feel?" Henry could say something like, "Mara, I feel frustrated when you grab stuff if you don't get your way" (I-message.) In the process of reframing the insulting label, he has given his big sister something useful to think about. And he may have even identified a bargaining chip for the mediation. Perhaps Mara will agree not to grab in exchange for getting Henry to agree to do something she wants him to do. (More about active listening and reframes in Chapter Nine.)

"You did that because you want to be the boss of everything." By presuming to know what made someone else do something, the speaker is making what mediators call an *attribution*. (Most people find attribution incredibly exasperating: how can someone else presume to know what motivates *me*?) I would try to get things back on track with a reframe: "Elizabeth, it sounds like you want to have some choices and make some of the decisions about how you and Katherine play shoe store (active listening.) Please tell her what she's doing that bothers you and how it makes you feel." Elizabeth might tell her sister, "I feel like I don't want to play with you when you don't let me choose stuff" (I-message). She has reframed her attribution, with two good, solid results. First, she has stopped trying to get inside her sister's head, which is both insulting and annoying. Second, she has targeted a behavior, so now they have something concrete to negotiate about. (More about attribution in Chapter Nine.)

A good rule of thumb when you are mediating is this: whenever one of the parties breaks a ground rule, calmly remind him about his commitment and assist him with a reframe. It's critically important to protect the mediation process, and maintaining a respectful tone serves that goal.

WORK AT POWER-BALANCING

It's not often that two people entering into mediation feel in every way like peers. A skillful mediator uses power-balancing techniques in order to neutralize obvious differences in rank or power. With natural imbalances suspended in this way, the parties can mediate on a level playing field as the equal human beings that they are. Balancing power is what Martin Luther King Jr. may have had in mind when he quoted Isaiah 40:4 in his landmark "I Have a Dream" speech: "Every valley shall be exalted, every hill and mountain shall be made low, the rough places will be made plain, and the crooked places will be made straight." Biblical scholars tell us that this verse is about removing obstacles, and I believe Dr. King re-purposed the quote to embrace fairness and justice.

There are so many ways in which siblings can be out of balance. These include:

- Age
- Size
- Strength
- Maturity level (as distinguished from age)
- Temperament (personality)
- Emotional expressiveness
- Verbal skill
- Ability/disability
- Self-control

A first power-balancing step is your decision about who should go first. Getting the chance to speak first can help someone who feels powerless or agitated to get a grip on things. Even how you address the children is important. Be aware of the use of nicknames. When mediating, it won't do to call your older son Arthur and his younger brother Booboo. It's either "Arthur and Bob" or "Artie and Booboo" — no mix and match!

Pay close attention to their body language. This may be your guide in helping kids dial it up or down. Jennifer may have expounded in loud and emphatic terms about a conflict with her younger sister Natalie, and all Natalie can come up with is "I'm mad" — even though it's obvious from her posture and expression that she is seething with rage. You may need to help her with words that match what you sense she is truly feeling: "It looks like this has made you absolutely *furious*." Then re-state what Jennifer has said in brief, slightly less dramatic terms. By re-writing their statements in the same font, so to speak, you help them feel equally valued and heard.

You may have to translate. The more mature or verbal child can overwhelm a sibling with words. Being clever with language gives her a lot of power; the less articulate sibling may feel like his sister is armed with a cannon whereas all he has is a slingshot. By simplifying what the highly verbal child says, and upgrading the terms of the less verbal one, you accomplish two things. First, you validate their feelings and opinions as having equal weight. Second, you enable the children to better hear and understand each other. Communication is maximized when differences in sophistication are minimized.

An older (or shrewder) child may be able to sell her sibling on a plan that is not in that sibling's best interest. If you catch the scent of unfairness in the air, first check to make sure you're not just reacting to "kid justice," which can sound very different from the "even-Steven" approach we adults usually strive for. If you're quite certain that one of them is being snowed, try asking *what-if* questions in order to gently unveil the unfairness. This is a key part of the Organization phase of mediation. If that fails, you may want to build a re-check into the contract, such as meeting in a week to see how things are going, and to re-open negotiations if necessary. "Live and learn" is a great teacher! Just remember that the balance between your personal sense of fairness and the need to remain neutral can be a delicate one. You can't really mediate if you are over-protecting one of the parties.

A last thing to keep in mind is that the adoration a younger sibling may feel for the older brother or sister is usually not reciprocated. Little kids usually look up to older kids. From the older child's perspective, it may appear something like this:

- *I feel pestered by him.* (I experience his attentions, questions and requests as annoying)
- *He must enjoy pestering me.*
- *Therefore he's a pest.*

The symmetry is just not there. It's hard for an older child to imagine what a thrill it is for the younger sibling to be included, heard, and respected by him. This is not an easy playing field for a parent to level, but anything you can do to develop this insight (without guilt or pressure, which usually backfire) can be very helpful.

### Look Under and Behind Feelings

Help the kids look for the feeling *before the feeling*. Children tend not only to be very general about the emotions they are experiencing ("I feel bad"), but they also tend to latch on to the last thing felt rather than the sequence of emotions that got them there. Look for ways to help them uncover their tracks:

- "Can you remember how were you feeling before you got mad?"
- "What was it like for you just before you scattered the puzzle?"
- "Did you notice anything happening for you before you said that?"

Once, in a seminar given by mediator Kenneth Cloke, we dissected a scenario in which a mother had lost track of her child in a busy department store. The child is happily hiding in one of the rounders, surrounded by puffy winter jackets. Within moments, the mother's curiosity ("where's Jared?") turns to anxiety and then stark terror. Loudly, she calls out his name. He pops out — "Surprise!" — and Mom is immediately flooded by anger. Curious about this rush of contrasting emotions, we role-played a conversation:

Ken: Why were you suddenly angry?

Mom: He had no right to scare me like that!

Ken: Why were you scared?

Mom: Because I couldn't find him.

Ken: What frightened you about that?

Mom: I was afraid of losing him!

Ken: And why were you afraid of losing him?

Mom: Because I love him!

Unpeeling anger revealed fear, and fear took us back to loss, and loss took us back to love. Retracing the rush of feelings that Mom had experienced, we hacked our way through the underbrush of all the most primal emotions.

Besides the feeling before the feeling, look for the feeling *under the feeling*. What are you hearing beneath their words? I want to share a tip, and it is just that — a tip — rather than a hard and fast rule. Children have great cultural antennae, and it doesn't take them long to figure out which emotions they have been conditioned to understand as acceptable for their gender. (This is changing, thank goodness, but emotional stereotyping is still very much a part of the social landscape.) In males, emotions that are perceived as weak, such as sadness or fear, often lurk under anger. In females, sadness often acts as a mask for anger or resentment. ("Nice little girls" aren't supposed to get mad or feel bitter, but it's OK for them to cry.) Helping kids unmask is a gentle process. It's not easy to do, and it takes a light touch. But it can yield rich rewards, both in terms of moving mediation along and helping children develop self-awareness. Additionally, it lets them know that they are entitled to experience the full range of human emotions. Despite cultural constraints, boys do get scared, and girls do get angry, and that's all right. We can't deal effectively with our emotions if we don't own them.

## SEPARATE POSITIONS FROM INTERESTS

People in conflict, whether they are children or adults, get very attached to their positions. In the book *Getting to Yes*, which for several decades has been the go-to handbook for negotiators, authors Roger Fisher, William Ury, and Bruce Patton discuss this in some detail. They define a position as what you believe you have to have. An interest is why you think so — the needs, desires, concerns, and fears that inform and drive a position. They tell us that, "the most powerful interests are basic human needs," which they list as follows (I have added my own kid-focused interpretations in italics):

- Security: *I need to feel loved and protected*
- Economic well-being: *I need my stuff — food, clothes, toys and so forth*
- A sense of belonging: *I need to feel like a cherished and valued member of the family*
- Recognition: *I need to be validated and have my feelings honored*
- Control over one's life: *I need to learn to express my feelings and to own my actions*

The path to these underlying interests is paved with good questions. In a classic mediation story used to illustrate the difference between position and interest, a farmer and a designer and a cook are squabbling over the grocer's last pumpkin. Each of the three characters is fused with his position: *I absolutely have to have this pumpkin.* The grocer asks them curious, open questions to get at the interests.

- "You really want the pumpkin badly. Can you tell us a little more about that?"
- "This pumpkin has a lot of meaning and importance to you. Why is that?"
- "What would you do with the pumpkin if you got it?"

Probing in this way, the grocer learns that the farmer wants the seeds for planting, the designer wants the shell for a jack-o'-lantern, and the cook wants the pulp for a pie. Listening to each other talk, the three disputants share a light bulb moment. The solution is a quirky (but entirely fair and satisfactory) three-way division of the pumpkin instead of a winner-take-all outcome.

Now of course it's rare for a real-life conflict to have such a tidy resolution. However, the story illustrates how important it is to question the *why I want it* underlying the *what I want*. Positional bargaining of the "I want it" / "No, I want it" type is a non-starter. This is why Fisher, Ury, and Patton flatly state, "focus on interests, not positions" and "don't bargain over positions."

Getting the parties detached from their positions and talking about their interests can really change the game in two important ways. First, the parties discover overlapping interests, which nudges them toward the same side of the problem-solving equation. Second, it has a softening effect. Once they warm to one another's interests, they problem-solve more readily. We saw this in Section 11 of Chapter Three, "The Keys to the Car." The older sister, Amira, had been annoyed by Ashley's insistence on her position ("I have to have the car") because it didn't make sense to her and because of a suspicion that important information was being withheld. Feeling annoyed and shut out just made her cling more stubbornly to her insistence that they drive together. Once Ashley divulged her reason for wanting the car, Amira understood the situation perfectly and backed down from her position with grace and ease.

## IDENTIFY OVERLAPPING THEMES AND INTERESTS

Be on the lookout for similarities in what children say they want. Even when it seems obvious to you that they want pretty much the same thing, or that they have similar reasons for wanting it, it's almost always worthwhile getting them to express this similarity in clear terms. Shared themes, sometimes referred to as overlapping interests, can provide a spark of empathy. These insights can act as softeners, nudging children a little closer to the "you and me against the problem" frame of mind. This is true even if the disagreement is hard to distinguish from the theme, which often happens with very young children (as when they are arguing over a toy.) Invite each of them to talk about why they like the toy so much. They may react warmly to one another's description. This in itself can help them feel less like adversaries and more like a team with a problem to solve. Highlighting overlapping wants might look like this, in three different age ranges:

- Preschool age: "I can see you both really enjoy special time alone with the blocks"
- School age: "What I'm hearing is you both really love having control of the remote"
- Teen: "It sounds like both of you want to discuss and maybe re-set some boundaries"

The first two look pretty obvious; the pairs of kids are arguing over a thing, and wanting that thing *is* the theme. Or is it? The parent has done a little subtle digging. The preschoolers are arguing over the blocks because they each find it so fun to play *alone* with them. The school-age siblings both want the remote but the core interest (or theme) may be *control*. In the first instance, the theme is autonomy; in the second, it's power.

As kids get older, it gets even more complicated — and yes, I know that's not exactly a news flash! In the case of the teenagers, Jerome might be complaining about what Jackson *does* (leaving stuff on Jerome's bed, for example) whereas Jackson is bothered by something Jerome *says* (such as insulting language.) The parent has figured out that the theme is "boundaries." Although the behaviors are quite different (action versus speech) they provoke exactly the same response: indignation. By identifying a common thread that defines and describes both behaviors, the parent is steering the teenagers toward an understanding that they each get irritated when the other one crosses a line.

## BE ON THE LOOKOUT FOR SOFTENERS

At the outset of mediation, typically both parties are very attached to their positions — their respective ideas of what they *must have* to feel better. The more intense someone's emotion is — anger, resentment, frustration — the tighter a grip she will probably have on her position. Anything that loosens that grip is a softener. Any acknowledgment of overlapping theme or interest, discussed at length in the previous section, can be a softener.

Other kinds of softeners include a compliment, an apology, a concession, an admission, or something of the sort. These cost nothing but could mean a lot to the other side. In fact, they can be powerful game-changers. If a gesture of this type seems to go unnoticed, you as mediator can retrieve and highlight it for the person to whom it was addressed:

"I just heard an apology. I'm wondering how that strikes you."

"It sounds like Hannah is willing to pay her half. Perhaps you have some thoughts about that."

"What I heard is that Rafael is taking responsibility for doing that. I'm curious to know how that makes you feel, now that he has stopped denying that he did it."

Note that none of these gambits *demands* a response, which is good. The mediator has spotlighted the apology (or concession, or admission) without insisting that the listener forgive, agree to the concession, or show gratitude for the admission. The mediator has led the horse to water without trying to force him to drink. And sometimes that's the best one can do.

### ATTEMPT TO GET THE PARTIES SIDE-BY-SIDE

In the beginning of mediation, it's best to have the kids facing one another, so they have full access to the visual cues provided by facial expression and body language. This maximizes good communication. You also don't want any physical lashing-out. If the kids are very young or very impulsive, you might want to have them sit a few feet apart, or across a kitchen table or coffee table. However, once the strong emotions have been discharged and you are moving into the Brainstorm phase, it's often a good idea to re-position them side-by-side. This makes the idea of "you and me against the problem" visible and concrete. Look for any reason to make a list, invent a chart or create some other graphic representation (a map of their bedroom, say.) Provide them with paper and crayons or pencils — whatever is appropriate. Working side-by-side harnesses whatever cooperativeness has been generated in the mediation, and it keeps the kids focused on a joint solution. In *Getting to Yes*, Fisher, Ury, and Patton write, "Like two shipwrecked sailors in a lifeboat at sea quarreling over limited rations and supplies, negotiators may begin by seeing each other as adversaries ... seeing themselves as engaged in side-by-side efforts to solve a mutual problem, the sailors will become better able to reconcile their conflicting interests as well as to advance their shared interests." Side-by-side behavior is enhanced when people are seated that way — literally.

### EMBRACE SILENCE

Silence is awkward. When you are running a meeting — and mediation is a meeting, after all — you naturally want it to go smoothly. But if you let go of the feeling that it's your responsibility to rescue everyone from these clumsy moments by plugging all the gaps, you can allow the awkwardness of silence to work toward getting to a solution. The silence that is making you squirm is also hard for the kids, and they may leap into the void. Sometimes if a direct question hasn't produced any results, a vague declarative statement, left hanging, will do the trick. Try dropping one into the air and then settle back in your chair as though you have all the time in the world. Look both kids in the eye. Remember that not all questions have answers, and that not all prompts are questions.

- "I wonder why this is so hard to talk about ... "
- "I wish we had some suggestions about solutions that might work ... "
- "I'm really interested in this argument but I don't understand it very well ... "

### Ensure That the Agreement Is "Durable and Do-Able"

Sometimes toward the conclusion of mediation, there is a tendency to overreach in making promises or providing assurances. In the happy glow of reconciliation, it's easy to overlook segments of a pact that are unrealistic. These can include matters out of the control of the parties, or they might involve people who aren't present at the mediation:

- "I will make Timothy stop teasing you"
- "I promise to play chess with you every Monday night"
- "Ms. Jackson will pay you the fine on your library book that James Jackson turned in late"

This is the point at which a good mediator has to be a bit of a party-pooper, coming up with exceptions and "what ifs." Be prepared to help your kids dial back their commitments to include only actions they can realistically accomplish and take responsibility for. This is the goof-proofing function of the Organization stage of mediation. Be sure no one is speaking for a party who is not there, or whose behavior is beyond his control:

- "I will tell Timothy that I want him to stop teasing you"
- "I will play chess with you every Monday night except when Mr. Hernandez gives us extra homework"
- "I'll ask Ms. Jackson to cover the fine on the book James borrowed and returned late"

It's also a good idea to engage the kids in a verbal walk-through of new behaviors they are promising to try. If there was a construction project going on in your neighborhood and you wanted your child to walk to school using a different route than his usual one, you might walk with him from your house to school along the new route. Doing that, rather than just describing the alternative route, would reduce the likelihood of his getting lost. A "rehearsal" of this kind begins to etch a new pattern in his brain. Questions that stimulate a mental walk-through of new behavior can help in the same way:

- "You've promised to give Leon more choices when you play together. What will that look like?"
- "What are some things you could do when you think your idea is better than Leon's?"
- "If you feel yourself starting to get impatient, what could you say? What could you do?"

## MANAGE PHYSICAL NEEDS

You are acutely aware of your children's needs — hunger, toileting, physical activity, etc. Mediation needn't be dry or stuffy, and it doesn't have to feel like a board meeting. If it's snack time, serve snacks. If one or both of the kids is restless, let them take a break to do jumping jacks or run around the couch ten times.

Reassure anyone who is leaving the room to exercise or go to the bathroom that you and the other party will take a break from the discussion while he is gone. Then keep your promise.

Sometimes very young children can focus better if you give them something to fiddle with, such as crayons and paper. (Maybe they can draw how they feel, or illustrate what the situation looks like to them, and then talk about it.) Slightly older kids can write down their thoughts and possible solutions as the mediation progresses. Sometimes taking notes helps a party focus on what the other is actually saying, instead of just formulating a rebuttal. But doodling is also fine; some people concentrate better that way. It probably goes without saying, but texting, answering calls, or anything distracting to the relational brain functions so fully deployed in mediation, are a no-no. This goes for the mediator as well as the parties.

A mediator I know always keeps a bowl of candy in her office. She brings it out whenever a resolution is close at hand but in danger of derailment because everyone is getting fidgety and cranky. And all of her clients are adults!


PEEL THE ONION

To beginning mediators, it sometimes doesn't make sense to deal with the "last thing first." We have an innate impulse to try to re-create a narrative in sequence, proceeding from beginning to middle to end. We are also naturally curious to know *how things started.* However, as we saw in Chapter Five, the parties themselves may not remember how it started, or they might have conflicting ideas about who fired the first shot. Jamila may be furious at Anthony for calling her a cheater just a few minutes ago when they were playing cards. However, he may still be smarting over something rude she said to him way last week. If you begin with the "cheater" remark, it's a good bet Anthony will at some point take the conversation back to last week's insult. A dispute can have lots of layers, like an onion. At first, the two kids (as well as the parent) can only see the outside layer: Anthony has called Jamila a cheater, and she is angry. Working backward may take the parties (as well as their mediator) into some unexpected territory, but it is actually a more natural and logical way to proceed.

## FOCUS ON PROCESS, DISREGARD SCALE

Parents often tell me they are baffled and exasperated about the smallness of things their kids argue about. Let's say your two children have been to a birthday party where they both received trinkets — two identical green key chains — in their goodie bags. Inevitably, one key chain has shown up and the other is missing. Both kids claim the found key chain, and they are squabbling over it for dear life. You're thinking, *good grief, it's only a key chain. Little kids don't even need key chains. They don't drive, and they're never locked out of the house! How could this possibly be worth my time?*

For starters, keep in mind that there will always be a gap between what you think is important and what your kids think is important. Two of my favorite comic strips are "Baby Blues" and "Zits." Ninety percent of what's funny in these strips takes place right on the divide between the adult agenda and the kid agenda. That gap will narrow considerably as your children mature, but it will always be there.

And the truth is that when they care and you don't, it's the *best* time to mediate. Their passion and your disinterest are actually the perfect combination! The kids are very invested, so they will stay focused and try hard. And it will be easy for you to stay neutral. What they will learn in resolving the conflict through mediation is much more important than The Fate of the Green Key Chain. Another way to say this is that the process (negotiating and problem-solving) is much more valuable than the product (a resolution.) People can learn and practice good negotiation skills whether they are arguing over a key chain or a huge real estate deal.

## EXPECT AN ICEBERG

Mediators often talk about "surfacing issues." To surface an issue is to conduct a conversation in such a way as to allow bigger and deeper concerns to be revealed so they can be discussed. In a way, doing this is counterintuitive. We already have a dispute on our hands — why make a mess even messier by expanding its scope or delving into the past? The reason is that mediation isn't really effective — in fact, it's not really mediation — if we just paper over a conflict. Having the courage (and patience) to look below the tip of the iceberg can yield long-term rewards. With siblings, who are SWOAPS as I've said before, old resentments usually produce lots of conflicts of the theme and variation type. When you notice that your kids are having a lot of little squabbles that center on the same theme, or any time someone seems really distressed over a seemingly small thing, you are wise to suspect that there is something below the iceberg's tip that's worth exploring.

### Use the Parking Lot

Sometimes parties in a negotiation will go off on a tangent. There are a lot of reasons for this. It could be a strategic distraction, like a cross-accusation that seems to come from out of left field. It could be due to restlessness, impulsiveness, self-absorption, or distractibility, all of which are abundant in early childhood. Or it could be the result of non-linear thinking ... "this reminds me of that, even though I can't say why." One way to manage these tangents, without going off in a million directions at once, is to use the Parking Lot: "That's a really interesting point, but I'd like us to finish discussing the bathroom schedule first. Let's put that in the Parking Lot and come back to later."

Write down the idea on a sheet marked Parking Lot. Do this no matter how wacky or unrelated the idea seems. Respect is the key. If time doesn't allow you to return to this as part of the present mediation, arrange with the kids before they are done to meet again and address it. But don't be surprised if this issue turns out to be a non-starter. If it was just a ruse or a distraction in the first place, interest in it will evaporate once the conflict gets resolved.

Jeff used the Parking Lot to good effect in Section 2 of Chapter Three, "A Room of One's Own." One of the issues he parked came from his younger daughter ("Who is Eva?"). The other was something that struck him in passing — Sylvia's hurt look when Sasha mentioned "privacy." Both issues made their way from the Parking Lot back to the mediation, with good results.


## ACKNOWLEDGE THE CORKSCREW

Sometimes in mediation, there arise several issues which the parties will address in a sort of rotation. It's a curious thing to observe. When one topic becomes too hot or uncomfortable, they move on to one of the others, often until they have made the circuit a number of times. Eventually one party, thoroughly exasperated, exclaims, "We're just going around and around!" *Or are they?*

There's a famous mediation called "The Purple House Mediation." It's well known in conflict resolution circles for a number of reasons. It forms the centerpiece of a landmark publication called *The Promise of Mediation* by Robert A. Baruch Bush and Joseph P. Folger. It has been transcribed and re-enacted as a training film. Its iconic status probably has a lot to do with the fact that the matters it addresses — ethnicity and race relations, private property, self-determination — are each issues commonly found at the heart of conflict. And here they are, all together in one epic struggle! When reading it, my initial reaction was "Oh dear, they're just going around and around." Then I noticed a strange thing. Each time the parties addressed one of the several sub-topics in their dispute, they went a little deeper. Then, having probed dangerously close to the bone, they would move on. It was as if by changing the subject they could get a little relief from the poking and prodding. When they returned to the topic, their beginning point was more intimate and honest than when they had discussed it before. In other words, they would leave a topic that had become sore, but when they returned to it they were (strangely, I thought) able to pick up slightly beyond where they had left off.

They weren't just going around and around. They were going deeper too. I had to think that somehow the circling was providing relief, a few minutes to heal and prepare for further probing.

I was reminded of a corkscrew. Yes, it goes around and around, but it also drills down further with each pass, thereby ultimately releasing the cork, the thing that blocks the neck of the bottle. This metaphor has sustained me whenever I hear that familiar "we're just going around and around" complaint. It allows me to agree while putting in my two cents' worth about what I think is really happening.

Let's look at two neighbors arguing about their property line. One of them, Bruce, says in exasperation, "We're just going around in circles!" I might say, "Yes, Bruce, I agree, we have been circling around from topic to topic. And here's something curious — I've noticed that each time, we get a little closer to things that really matter." Then I give an example specific to the mediation at hand: "The first time you expressed your annoyance about the rose bushes, Elaine told you that they were planted by her mother just after her father died. Elaine got kind of emotional, and you responded with kindness and understanding. It was a sort of touching moment, and soon after, the subject changed to the rear wall. But when we returned to the issue of the rose bushes, you both looked a lot calmer and were able to begin doing some problem-solving. Is that how you experienced it too?"

So when things are going round and round, see if you notice the "corkscrew effect." That may be what's happening. If not, and the conversation is merely repetitious, some of the techniques in "Work Through Impasse" and "Caucus With the Parties" (below) or "Embrace Silence" (earlier in this chapter) might help. As a final resort, when someone is truly stuck in a repetitive pattern, try asking in a firm tone, "Is there anything *new* that we haven't already talked about?" Once nothing new is offered, insist on moving on to the next stage of mediation.

## ESCROW THE TOY

When two kids are fighting over property (the remote, a toy, a book, etc.) I suggest holding it or putting it aside while the mediation is in progress. It's really hard for a child to calm down and think straight when the thing he desperately wants is right in the hands of his opponent. This is what Samuel did when he took possession of the truck in Section 6 of Chapter Three, "The Young and the Restless." Once the mediation is over and the kids have made a very specific plan for sharing the thing, you can hand it over as appropriate. Hint: if you aren't sure whom to hand it to, you still need to complete the goof-proofing (Organization) stage of mediation. You're not done until the kids have a plan that picks up right where the mediation leaves off.

## Caucus if Necessary

Mediators use the term "caucus" to refer to the practice of separating the parties during mediation. In my own practice, I use caucusing very sparingly. However, on the occasions when intuition tells me to meet privately with the disputants, this almost always yields rich and interesting results. And I should add that, on the few occasions when I thought to caucus and decided against it, I have usually regretted that decision. I would say that trusting your gut is the best guide. If you suspect that there's something unsaid or locked-in that isn't coming to the surface, you may well be right. We have intuition for a reason — feel free to use it!

Caucusing often helps when things get stuck. *Always* caucus with both parties even if you only seek information from one of them; this preserves feelings of trust. Before caucusing, tell them you want to see them both privately and that anything they say to you will be kept in confidence if they want it that way. When caucusing, your job is to listen, not to reason with them or give advice. You can begin each of the private sessions by saying something along the lines of "I just thought it might be good to talk with each of you individually. Is there something on your mind?"

Caucusing can be helpful in a lot of ways. For example, if one of the kids is unresponsive to the other, or remains negative about the process of mediating, you can use the caucus to reality-check: *What's your best alternative to solving the problem this way? How do you think this will get solved if the mediation breaks down? Where will that leave you?* Or perhaps one of the kids is extremely tense or angry. Maybe both are. The opportunity to vent and to be warmly heard by a neutral party might provide enough calm for the mediation to be resumed successfully. And sometimes there's a declaration or disclosure that one party wasn't comfortable making in front of the other.

In this last case, you and the child have some important things to consider: whether to bring it up in mediation, and if so, packaging it for optimal impact, and possibly rehearsing how to say it. This is coaching in its lightest form, not a time to step out of the mediator role with advice, opinions, or cues. Try to keep the good questions coming. Does the child want to share these ideas with the sibling? Sometimes just getting things off his chest with you is enough. Reassure the child that you will keep this confidential if that's his wish. But if the child wants to bring the ideas or feelings to the mediation and simply doesn't know how, you can use the caucus time to rehearse how things could go and to explore possible outcomes.

Your daughter might say, "I want to talk to Alice about the mess in our closet, but every time I bring it up she starts yelling." You can ask what the child might say before bringing up the messy closet, how she thinks it would be best to talk about the "mess," how she can plan to react if Alice does in fact start hollering. When you help a child hone her conflict skills in this way, caucusing can serve as a kind of backstage run-through. This is especially helpful for the child who is risk-averse, more inclined to back down than engage in a heated dispute. Exploring a question like "What's the worst thing that can happen?" sometimes helps a person realize that her worst fear is something she can in fact handle. Mediation — and within mediation, the opportunity to caucus — provides this child with rehearsal space wherein she takes greater control and learns to advocate for her needs.

## DEPEND ON A DO-OVER

One process that can really benefit from percolation is the Do-Over. Sometimes, the circumstances just aren't right for the level of follow-through necessary to achieve a resolution. Time runs out, the parties are too emotional to continue, people get discouraged or lose focus. A do-over really can work. It's up to you whether to take up where you left off or start back at the beginning. I would lean toward the latter option if intuition tells you that things went badly because you missed a step in the TABMOC protocol, or if feelings were still very intense when everybody gave up. If, on the other hand, the mediation only ended because of time constraints or simple "engine failure," you could probably just start where you left off. Engage the parties to help you paint a picture of what that looked like ("What have we got so far?") to get everybody on the same page, and to make sure no false assumptions are in play. (We saw a do-over in Chapter Three, Section 11. Since Take One had ended with an angry walkout, Leon was smart to begin at the beginning in mediating Take Two.)

WORK THROUGH IMPASSE

"Impasse" is the word mediators use to describe getting stuck in mediation. Sometimes you just get to a point where no one will budge or the parties run out of suggestions they can negotiate over. One technique I use when I hit the wall is caucusing, above. Two others are "Embrace Silence" and "Depend on a Do-Over," discussed earlier in this chapter. Further techniques that sometimes work for getting through impasse are:

- Postponing to another day or a later time that same day
- Taking a short break (this could be a nap, bathroom stop, or exercise session)
- Serving a snack
- Asking a really bold question ("What would it take to reach an agreement?")
- Saying "I'm really stuck (puzzled, confused, etc.) Can you help me out?"
- Reviewing the mediation so far

This last one is important because it takes you back to the TABMOC protocol. Really take your time and recap everything that was said so far. You may discover that you skipped a step or scooted past something important. Also, hearing a review of the mediation so far may jog a memory or spotlight something yet unsaid. Going back to pick up these lost pieces can sometimes recharge a stalled mediation.

Mediators talk about a BATNA and a WATNA. A BATNA is the "best alternative to a negotiated agreement." WATNA, of course, is the worst. Ask both kids to consider the best and worst outcome if they don't figure out something together. The BATNA might be, "She'll give me the doll." How likely is that? (Fat chance.) The WATNA might be, "She'll keep the doll, and I won't have anyone to play with besides." Thinking about these bleak scenarios can really get the juices flowing!

If none of these techniques breaks the impasse, and you have to end mediation, try not to end on a note of defeat. You can say, "Well, we didn't reach a conclusion today, but you both worked hard on this. I appreciate the patience and effort you put into it. I really learned a lot, and I hope you did too!" After that, *trust percolation*.


## TRUST PERCOLATION

I really can't emphasize this enough. As any coffee lover knows, you don't get a good cup of coffee without the steeping process. Just as hot water seeps ever so slowly through those ground beans to produce a rich, satisfying brew, people's thoughts and feelings percolate too. Our everyday experiences remind us that this is so. At work, Omar offers Marcie a suggestion, a request or an observation, and Marcie gets a little defensive. The conversation ends awkwardly. There's a touch of rancor in the air. Omar takes away the feeling that it was a complete waste of time, maybe even damaging to the relationship. Later, when the pressure is off, Marcie mulls over (consciously and/or unconsciously) what was said. The result is that a week or a month later, there is a change in Marcie's outlook and behavior. She may actually believe that the idea to change came entirely from within — because to her, it actually feels that way. Omar is astonished by the change, coming as it does after a gap in time and without further observable processing. This is certainly not an outcome that looked likely at the conclusion of that awkward conversation!

Ending mediation with a question (or a prompt for the parties themselves to be inquisitive) can stimulate percolation. A vague pronouncement like "I'm wondering why [such-and-such], and I want to think a little more about that" invites others to ponder with you without pressuring them for an instant reply. Rescheduling the mediation for a day or a week later takes good advantage of everyone's capacity for percolation. Or perhaps the mediation ends inconclusively, and there is no plan to reconvene. In either case, ending with a question conveys optimism, curiosity, and confidence rather than dismay.

## BE PATIENT WITH YOURSELF

Mediating is a little daunting. Allow yourself time and practice to get comfortable in this new role. Deciding to try mediation might feel like you are giving yourself a demotion! Instead of functioning in an executive role:

- Judge
- Adviser
- Arbitrator
- Decision-maker
- Expert
- Umpire
- Referee

You are taking on a supporting role:

- Observer
- Listener
- Questioner

- Secretary
- Timekeeper
- Reflector/Mirror
- Interpreter
- Cheerleader

Even the questions you are asking have a childlike quality — naive and openhearted rather than fact-finding or accusatory. By taking a step back, you give your children the chance to step up. They will learn to deal with conflict responsibly and competently.

Be assured that as mediator you maintain control. You will not determine the outcome, but you will exercise your authority and preserve the process by making sure the parties follow the protocol, observe the agreed-upon ground rules, and honor the terms of their contract.

# 7

# DECIDING WHEN TO MEDIATE AND WHEN TO ARBITRATE

*B*y now it's obvious that I'm a big fan of mediation. But it's equally obvious that you can't mediate every dispute — or even every other dispute. Nor should you. Once or twice a week may be all the traffic you can bear. Often, kids can just work things out themselves. It's when they are stuck, or really struggling, or when things are heating up to the boiling point that they may need you to step in. So how to decide whether to mediate or arbitrate?

### WHEN TO MEDIATE

For me, the gold standard is *I don't have a dog in this fight.* If you are unconcerned about the outcome, consider mediating. In a way, everything having to do with your kids has to do with you. However, lots of issues arise that the kids care about deeply that *don't* include you as a stakeholder. Those are great times to mediate. Conflicts about sharing time, space, and resources crop up frequently in families. Even if you confine yourself to these types of situations, you will have ample opportunity for mediation. Beyond that, an answer of "yes" to any of these questions might help you decide in favor of mediation:

- Is this issue chronic? (lasting over time)
- Is it repetitious? (recurring and centering on a single idea or want)
- Does it resonate with other conflicts these two have been having? ("theme and variation")
- Am I having trouble understanding what's really going on? ("tip of the iceberg")

## WHEN TO ARBITRATE

I would arbitrate rather than mediate when:

- Time is short
- Circumstances are unfavorable (e.g., you are in traffic and need to focus on driving)
- You are in a bad mood or your patience is wearing thin
- You are too angry to do a good job of mediating
- You are feeling certain that there's a "perp" and a "vic" (i.e., you just can't be neutral)

I want to say more about that fifth and last example. There could be any number of reasons why you might not feel neutral about a conflict your kids are having. It could just be that Gabby was picking on Tony all day Tuesday, so you didn't even start your day feeling very neutral on Wednesday. Or it could be because one of your kids has actually done something that breaks a family rule. If that's the case, then your primary challenge is about discipline, not helping them settle a squabble. (I talked about Discipline at the beginning of Chapter Six, but just to reiterate — when I use that term I mean teaching, not punishing.) Parents should always be on the lookout for teachable moments. In fact, what *is* good parenting if not a long string of teachable moments? Your kids' development of an ethical system rests squarely with you. If your child has done something that violates your family's code, it's your job to step up in a way that's firm and timely, while at the same time developmentally appropriate and compassionate.

But in cases like the first four in the list above — where you choose to arbitrate simply because of time constraints, unfavorable conditions, or because your mood isn't conducive to mediating — you could consider postponing mediation until the circumstances are right and / or you are feeling calmer and more centered. This is to say you might choose an "arb now, med later" approach: "OK, we're in a hurry to get to the dentist, So Harry you get in the front seat, and Howie I want you in the back. Tomorrow is Friday, and we won't have any homework pressure, so after school, let's sit down and look for a long-term solution to this Who Sits Where thing. Wouldn't it be great to settle it once and for all?"

Or not. Arbitrate when you think it's best. It's better to arbitrate well than to mediate badly. In addition, I would definitely choose to arbitrate in the following circumstances.

**Arbitrate when a decision calls for adult experience, judgment, and or/wisdom.** Kids, even older kids, don't always have the big picture, and like all of us they are motivated by self-interest. Often your adult perspective is required. Let's say a winter storm is raging and your sons (Daniel, 17 and Douglas, 16) have plans to drive to a town fifteen miles away to attend their school's basketball game. You're not thrilled about this situation, but you told them they could have the car for the evening and a promise is a promise. Naturally, they both want to drive. What you know is this: they are both pretty good drivers. Daniel, however, has a lead foot, and he takes more chances than Douglas. On the plus side, he is much better at navigating. With Douglas (the more circumspect and cautious driver) at the wheel and Daniel riding shotgun, you have the best of both worlds. You say something diplomatic like, "Doug, I want you to do the driving tonight. It will be good experience for you in this kind of weather. Dan, you be the navigator, and keep an eye on directions."

**Arbitrate when safety is an issue.** Babette is five-years-old and Nicole is three-years-old. The two sisters are playing in the living room.

They've invented a game of stacking cardboard blocks and knocking them down with a ball. You're getting a little worried that a wayward ball could knock over a lamp or a picture frame, but you have hesitated to interfere because the girls are having so much fun together. Now Babette wants to move to the kitchen floor (to make the stacking less frustrating), but Nicole is impatient to keep playing on the fluffy carpet, even though the stacking challenge is obviously making her grouchy. Babette clearly has the right idea from the standpoint of logistics, and you know that the activity will probably go more smoothly and last longer if some of the frustration can be dialed down. None of this, of course, is on Nicole's mind — after all, she's only three. You say, "I'm going to decide where I want you to play this game. I'll help you move all the blocks into the kitchen. The kitchen floor is better for stacking, *and* the knickknacks in the living room will be safe from the ball."

In closing, I would reiterate that outright arbitration of every conflict (in other words, acting as judge or referee every single time there is a dispute) may prevent kids from becoming conflict-competent. There are additional parent strategies that I think are worth mentioning here because they so closely resemble arbitration in the outcomes they produce.

## VERBAL SHUTDOWN

When parents proclaim a solution ("Be nice to your brother." or "Just give her the ball, she's younger than you."), they invalidate negotiation. This tells the kids that it's not worth taking the time to figure things out, and that children lack the ability to problem-solve. Directing a solution robs them of the opportunity to learn how to work things out. As such, it's a teachable moment missed. (More about this in the section on sharing in Chapter Nine.)

## ALWAYS SEPARATING SIBLINGS IN CONFLICT

Separating kids who are in conflict, or warming up to a conflict, is an attempt to short-circuit trouble. This usually just postpones the drama to a later time. They are fighting for a reason, and the reason doesn't just go away if you ignore or suppress it. You might have to separate children for safety reasons if tempers are high. However, you can bring the kids back together after they have calmed down enough to mediate.

### OVER-PROGRAMMING

Kids whose lives are chock-full of lessons and structured activities have very little "hanging out" time with their siblings. These children are spared the challenge of sharing space and materials. There may be less conflict, but where there is no conflict there can be no development of peacemaking skills. I would remind you that conflict is an opportunity. I actually think hanging out is undervalued. Having no agenda prompts children to be creative, to find their own strategies for keeping boredom at bay, to figure out what they actually enjoy doing together (and apart), to read, to discover — and, inevitably, to experience conflict and resolution.

### A TV IN EVERY ROOM

Buying two, three, and four of everything does reduce conflict. Unfortunately, it's also isolating. Consider limiting possessions for the very purpose of having your kids learn how to negotiate and share. Also consider giving them something you expect them to play with together. A very wise mom who was in one of my parenting classes told our group about the family she grew up in. She had seven brothers and sisters. Long on kids and short on cash, her parents gave them Christmas gifts that were expressly for sharing, like a toy stove or dollhouse. Working things out was a behavior that was embedded in their play, with very positive results.

### AVOIDING FAMILY MEALTIMES

Family life can be hectic, and mealtimes are sometimes stressful. It's easy to fall into the habit of skipping a sit-down family meal. But breaking bread with others is a civilizing and bonding experience —

and it's worth taking *whatever measures are needed* to sit down at least once a day with your family to share food and respectful conversation. Here's what cooking expert Marion Cunningham had to say on the subject: "The real key is sharing food at that table. And, believe me, we know we're not born civilized ... so you have to be taught the table is the place you learn who you are and where you're from ... you come to know one another. The result is you know who you are."

If a shared meal isn't possible, try to create another ritual for your family. It could be a hike, a visit to the farmers market or time spent at the park. The key features of a bonding experience are: enjoying a pleasant experience together, having relaxed and meaningful conversation, and unplugging from distractions such as electronic devices.

The five strategies I've just detailed can be conscious as well as unconscious efforts to purchase some peace and quiet. But *keeping the peace* is not the same as giving kids tools for *making peace*. Just be mindful that these strategies are actually decisions to avoid experiences that could be beneficial to your family. Ask yourself if you are getting a short-term gain (less fighting) at the expense of a long-term gain: conflict competence.

## 8

# COLLATERAL BENEFITS

*W*hat is the parent modeling when he mediates? And what do kids experience in the process? Mediation-savvy people learn quickly that a lot of the language and techniques they are deploying serve to oil the wheels of life in general. Because of this, I think of mediation as having collateral benefits. Having these words and these strategies allows you to talk to people more comfortably, to make your wants known, to negotiate skillfully, and to embrace compromise. These techniques simply smooth life's way. Mediation's collateral benefits are worth considering.

### "HEY THIS ACTUALLY WORKS!" I-MESSAGES AND ACTIVE LISTENING

Kids who mediate frequently learn by experience how effective I-messages and active listening can be. It's a relief to be able to share strong emotions in a way that reduces the likelihood that the person you are confronting will get angrier, become more defensive, or retaliate. It's an amazing experience to be able to calm an opponent (and who doesn't want a calmer opponent?) by showing some empathy for his or her situation.

Both I-messages and active listening are of course conciliatory —
but at the same time they are *empowering* because they give the child
some control over the tone of the conversation. With anger and
defensiveness cleared from the pathway, there's a better chance of
getting through to the other person and bringing about desired
outcomes. The child is impressed: *This works in my favor.* Though we
have to teach children the language of I-messages and active
listening (most successfully, by modeling), there isn't much need for
drilling or persuasion for the simple reason that these techniques
provide their own reward. They create a positive feedback loop, so
using them is both habit-forming and incredibly contagious. (More
about I-messages and active listening in Chapter Nine.)

### Self-Mastery (Emotion Regulation)

One of the chief tasks of childhood is developing self-control.
Mediation is an ideal setting for nurturing the ability to curb
impulsiveness. For one thing, there are ground rules: *If my opponent
doesn't fly off the handle, I probably won't either.* For another thing, it's a
win-win: *Because I have the expectation of getting some of what I want,
and because I'm not overanxious about losing everything, I will hang in
there and work on a solution.* Negotiating takes patience and self-
control, but kids learn that by staying reasonable and respectful, they
often attain the more satisfactory resolution. After all, if you get what
you want by wheedling, making a fuss, throwing a tantrum or
hurting someone, you do so at the expense of the other person's
cooperation and good will. You may get the truck (or the book, or the
doll) from your brother by means of one of theses negative
strategies, but now he doesn't want to play with you. One of the
lessons of mediation is that you can get some of what you want
while buttressing or repairing a relationship, instead of getting all of
what you want *at the expense of the relationship.* Accepting this trade-
off ("if I compromise, I will be rewarded") is a stunning milestone in
the socio-emotional life of a child.

Neuroscience tells us that emotional literacy (in this case, being able to identify and share the emotions we are feeling) is a key ingredient to emotional self-mastery. There is a saying: "If you can name it, you can tame it." The technique of identifying strong negative emotion is the keystone of anger management programs prescribed for adults who never mastered their rage. Not surprisingly, it works with little kids too — only much more easily, because children are so much more receptive and baggage-free. "Naming the feeling" has this regulating effect because the location in our brain where we experience strong emotions is different from the place where we identify and observe them. Neurologically speaking, you cannot *be furious* and *reflect upon your fury* at the same time. Negotiation expert Roger Fisher coined the term "go to the balcony" to capture this idea of stepping back from strong emotion in order to observe it. This is what we mean when we distinguish between the reactive brain and the reflective mind. Anger happens in the primitive core of the brain, but thinking about anger happens in the highly developed reaches of the mind. The view from the balcony is tall and broad. It offers perspective.

Whatever self-mastery we can muster helps us navigate conflict. We don't have to deny or suppress emotions in order to negotiate. Rather, we have to deploy them in a socially acceptable way. In mediation, children get to be altogether honest about their feelings while honoring the social rules that govern how those feelings can be expressed. This is really about distilling emotions for authenticity.

I have to say, a lot of what passes for emotion dysregulation in kids (lack of self control) looks staged to me. I'm not referring to early tantrums, the spontaneous ones that happen when toddlers are overwhelmed with feeling. I'm talking about what can happen if tantrums *pay off*. Children in conflict, just like their adult counterparts, sometimes carry on and engage in dramatic displays because they have learned that these strategies produce gratifying results. Parents and older siblings may give in to extravagant displays of emotion, because of annoyance or embarrassment. If inauthentic behavior results in a payoff, kids will keep on doing it. In mediation, children learn another, healthier way of getting their needs met. They learn that conflict doesn't have to be about fake dramatics. It's about genuine emotion: *I can let the other person know how their words or behavior affect me in order to move toward a mutually satisfactory resolution.* Counterfeit emotion is for the stage and screen, not the dinner table! The self-knowledge that flows from honest exploration of one's feelings will lead to self-mastery.


EMOTIONAL LITERACY

Some people are born with more emotional intelligence (ability to read others' emotions, capacity for empathy) than others, just as some children show early athletic talent or a gift for understanding numbers. This is in keeping with a theory developed by Howard Gardner in his book *Frames of Mind: The Theory of Multiple Intelligences.* Gardner broke ground because he exposed our educational system as favoring just a few intelligences (in particular, math/spatial and verbal) and because he widened the playing field to embrace numerous ways of being intelligent. As the saying — often misattributed to Albert Einstein — goes, "Everybody is a genius, but if you judge a fish by its ability to climb a tree, it will live its whole life believing that it is stupid."

Sometimes one hears the term "emotional intelligence" used to describe all the things one can *learn* in order to be more attuned to others. I find this confusing, so I use the term as Gardner does, reserving it to describe a person's natural, inborn capacity for emotion-reading and empathy. I use the term "emotional literacy" to encompass all the things we can teach and model to enhance a person's natural gifts (whether modest or impressive) for understanding emotions.

We see how this works in other intelligences. For example, one child shows an early aptitude for music; she picks out familiar tunes on the piano, makes up songs and adores listening to music. Her parents give her violin lessons. An obvious prodigy, she attends a music academy and winds up as concertmaster with a prestigious symphony orchestra. Another child shows an average amount of interest in music. She takes violin lessons for several years and sings with her high school choir. As an adult, she enjoys music and buys season tickets for the symphony. Both children, through music education, have built musical literacy upon their innate musical intelligence.

Emotional literacy works the same way. Some of us are born with extraordinary emotional intelligence, and most of us are not. However, we can all become emotionally literate. In experiences such as mediation, a child is reminded that his emotions matter. He also learns to be curious and respectful about other people's emotions. He discovers that feelings have names. Over time, he learns that emotions are nuanced; they vary in shading (worried, dreading, afraid) and intensity (annoyed, angry, furious). Probably the two most important emotional literacy gains offered by mediation are empathy-building and perspective-taking.

## EMPATHY-BUILDING

The heart of empathy is listening. It's surprisingly hard to *just listen* — to hear other people without judging or denying the feelings they express. (More about this in Chapter Nine, "Active Listening.") It's a challenge not to give in to the urge to fix things or try to change how another person feels. A mediator models this kind of listening and encourages the parties to do the same.

A skillfully conducted mediation offers both parties the chance to explore their own emotions as well as the feeling-states of their opponents. As each child grapples with the challenge of re-stating the other's position, both kids experience the relief of feeling heard. If the mediator is both neutral and warmly validating, both children see that all the emotions on the table are real and important. This way of hearing trains the ear, so to speak, to listen for *interests* that underlie *positions*. The unmasking of those interests can be a revelation, a real "aha!" moment: *She wants the same thing I do — and for pretty much the same reason!* (We looked at positions and interests in Chapter Six.)

Empathy-building doesn't just benefit the kids. When you mediate for your children, you become more intimately acquainted with them — the unique way each one processes feelings, the meaning behind gestures or behaviors. You may learn to read your kids more accurately. A relaxed, skillfully-conducted mediation can take you into unexpected territory. You get to know your kids better just as they come to understand and respect one another more deeply.

### PERSPECTIVE-TAKING

In conflict, it's very challenging to see the other person's point of view. It's "my way vs. the wrong way" or "your way vs. the right way." The more disordered a conflict is — for example, when tempers are rising out of control, when the stakes are very high, or when physical harm is imminent — the less likely it is that the parties can get a perspective on each other. Add to this the fact that young children are naturally and appropriately very egocentric. Mediation provides the structure to reduce disorder in conflict. It also provides built-in opportunities to listen for understanding and state the other person's position. These forays beyond egocentrism are tiny exercises that build the mind's capacity for perspective-taking just as surely as sit-ups build abdominal strength. I think the lessons of perspective-taking are threefold.

The first is that we all have our own truth. How we perceive an event and store it as a memory is a process that's personal and quirky. How often have you seen a movie with another person and walked out with two completely different impressions? Everything about the film — plot, motivation, character development — is seen through two different prisms, with the result that you and your companion have constructed two contrasting experiences of the movie. *The fact that you and I have a different memory of an event doesn't mean that one of us is lying.*

The second lesson of perspective-taking is that being able to restate what an opponent feels is not the same as backing down or agreeing with that person. We have an almost superstitious or magical fear of taking the opponent's perspective — as if by doing so, our own argument or position might crumble. What actually happens when Heather restates James' position is that James calms down and feels heard. As a consequence, James starts listening for understanding rather than listening just in order to argue back. The conversation deepens and becomes less adversarial. *Perspective-taking serves me as a strategic tool because it soothes my opponent and motivates him to hear me better.*

The third lesson has to do with how people feel about disagreement, especially in intimate relationships. It's dismaying how many adults have carried the egocentrism of childhood into this sphere. We've all known an adult who thinks this way: "If I can just find the right way to explain this, you will certainly see the rightness of my thinking." To this person, others disagree with him simply because he has not explained himself adequately or because they are not listening carefully enough. The truth is that sometimes disagreement is not due to a failure of communication. *You may understand me perfectly and yet never, ever see this my way.*

NEGOTIATION SKILL

You don't plan on tying your child's shoes for him on his wedding day — that's why you take the time to teach him how to tie his own shoes! Mediation works the same way. As we saw in Chapter One, mediation fosters conflict competence. Gradually and naturally, your children will wean themselves from needing your assistance. They will have a tool belt full of useful strategies for dealing with conflict. Moreover, they will know from experience that the strategies *really work*:

- Being respectful rather than combative
- Listening responsively rather than just crafting a heated rebuttal
- Asking "what are my underlying interests?"
- Being curious about the opponent's underlying interests
- Expecting to compromise in reconciling interests
- Offering something that costs nothing but has great

meaning for the opponent (an admission, an apology, a
compliment, the offer of a favor)

Skillful negotiators use these tools without even thinking about
them because the tools bring success, and your child will learn to
also. As these strategies become habitual conflict behaviors, your
child becomes conflict-competent.

# 9

# RELATIONSHIP TALK

*S*o far, I've focused on using the technique of mediation in the family — how it works, why I think it's a good practice, the benefits it provides. In this chapter, I'll talk about family communication more broadly. I hope to provide some ideas about fostering relationship talk 24/7, not just when conflict occurs. These practices not only set the scene for effective mediation when a dispute happens, but I think they also deepen each family member's capacity for relationship.

RICH EMOTION LANGUAGE

In my talks with parents of preschoolers, I often ask them to raise their hands if their children know the names of ten farm animals and the noises those animals make. Usually all the hands go up. Then I ask if their kids know the words for ten emotions. Nearly all of the hands go down. "When was the last time your child saw a duck or a cow?" We live in a huge urban center, so they strain to remember their last trip to a petting zoo. "But," I press, "when was the last time your child was sad or discouraged or thrilled or furious?" Without much prodding, the parents realize that there is in fact a good-sized cluster of emotions that young kids experience frequently if not multiple times daily.

Don't get me wrong; I have nothing whatsoever against introducing a child to farm animals. It's part of the canon we teach them — like naming colors and shapes, and counting from one to ten. And it's adorable to see a toddler point to a picture of a duck, proclaim that it's a "guck" and quack enthusiastically! I just want us to add emotion words to that canon. They are so useful, and they are so easily taught. When you are experiencing a strong emotion and someone names that emotion with empathy, you will immediately grasp its meaning. There is poignancy and comfort in the fact that there is a word for what you are feeling: *I am not alone; others have gone before me.* Having someone identify your emotion helps you understand that what you are experiencing is powerful and important. Brain science tells us that it also allows you to step out of that feeling, where you are immersed *in it*, and look *at it*. This sets in motion some of the mind's powerful mechanisms for regulating emotion.

I'm reminded of the time a mom brought her son to our Parent-Toddler class a little late. We were cleaning up after free play, and her son was devastated to realize he had missed the opening part of our morning. He sobbed inconsolably on his mother's shoulder. She was trying to comfort him in their home language, which happens not to be English. (Mom is bilingual, but her son didn't have much English yet.) Not being able to talk with him directly, I encouraged her to tell him "You are so disappointed," but she said that the word for *disappointed* (in their language) was too long. Another mom reminded her that her son knows Tyrannosaurus rex — and that's pretty long!

The challenging word for T. rex came easily to him because he is extremely interested in big, strong dinosaurs. The fact is, kids are very interested in big, strong emotions, too. They spend a lot of time engulfed in powerful feelings and struggling to process them. When we pair an emotion word with the experience a child is having, we are validating the child, empathizing with him, and giving him a useful communication tool. Words like "disappointed" and "frustrated" and "delighted" *are* big and important — but so are the feelings they describe.

Have a look at the list of emotion words listed in "Beyond Mad-Sad-Glad." The words are specific and varied. This is intended to be a fairly comprehensive list, useful for talking to grownups as well as children. But you will probably notice certain words that pop out at you because they are so familiar in the daily emotional life of kids. I encourage you to make a copy of the list with "the usual suspects" highlighted, and post it on the fridge as a reminder to use them daily. Or you could make a list of the commonest emotions in big letters so your kids can see them too.

### BEYOND MAD-SAD-GLAD

- Accepting, Resigned
- Affectionate, Caring, Loving
- Afraid, Alarmed, Fearful, Frightened, Scared, Terrified
- Aggravated, Bothered, Concerned, Disturbed
- Aggressive, Combative, Violent
- Agitated, Distraught, Distressed, Impatient, Nervous, On edge, Panicky, Restless, Uncomfortable, Uneasy, Upset
- Amazed, Astonished, Flabbergasted, Shocked, Startled, Stunned, Stupefied, Surprised
- Ambivalent, Conflicted
- Amenable, Easygoing, Flexible
- Amused, Funny, Giggly, Playful, Silly, Zany
- Angry, Annoyed, Enraged, Furious, Indignant, Inflamed, Infuriated, Mad, Provoked, Seething
- Anticipative, Expectant
- Anxious, Apprehensive, Concerned, Dreading, Troubled, Worried
- Apathetic, Avoidant, Detached, Indifferent, Uncaring, Unfeeling, Uninterested
- Appreciated, Cherished, Liked, Loved, Valued

- Aroused, Eager, Energetic, Enthusiastic, Excited, Exuberant, Overexcited, Passionate
- Ashamed, Shamed
- Attacked
- Baffled, Confused, Perplexed, Puzzled
- Belittled, Berated, Criticized, Degraded, Denied, Devalued, Discounted, Disrespected, Rejected, Unworthy
- Belligerent, Stubborn
- Betrayed, Cheated, Duped
- Bitter, Resentful
- Bold, Brave, Confident, Courageous, Sure
- Bored
- Burdened, Overwhelmed, Put-upon, Stressed
- Calm, Comfortable, Gentle, Patient, Peaceful, Quiet, Relaxed, Serene
- Cautious, Guarded, Hesitant, Insecure, Reluctant, Unsure, Wary
- Clingy
- Compassionate, Generous, Helpful, Kind
- Contemptuous
- Content, Contented, Delighted, Ecstatic, Elated, Glad, Happy, Joyful, Pleased, Thrilled
- Contrary, Oppositional, Rebellious
- Cranky, Fussy, Irascible, Irritable, Irritated, Hungry, Physically uncomfortable, Sleepy
- Curious
- Defeated, Intimidated, Overpowered, Pressured, Subjugated
- Dejected, Depressed, Despondent, Grief-stricken, Heartbroken, Inconsolable, Miserable, Mournful, Sad, Tearful, Unhappy
- Derided, Made fun of, Mocked
- Despairing, Helpless, Inadequate, Useless
- Desperate, Hopeless, Trapped
- Despised, Detested, Hated, Loathed
- Determined

- Devastated, Discouraged, Dismayed, Fed up
- Disappointed
- Disgusted, Repelled
- Disliked, Excluded, Ignored, Isolated, Lonely, Lonesome, Neglected, Unappreciated, Unliked, Unloved, Unrecognized
- Dissociative, Emotionless, Flat, Unemotional
- Distracted
- Doubtful, Doubting, Pessimistic, Skeptical
- Embarrassed, Mortified
- Engaged, Focused, Friendly, Interested, Involved
- Enticed, Tempted
- Envious, Jealous
- Exasperated, Frustrated
- Exhausted, Fatigued, Tired, Worn out
- Grateful, Gratified, Thankful
- Guilty
- Hopeful, Optimistic
- Humiliated, Hurt, Insulted, Offended
- Hysterical
- Independent
- Inspired, Motivated
- Longing, Wishful, Yearning
- Mischievous
- Nostalgic
- Possessive
- Powerful, Strong
- Protected, Safe, Secure
- Proud, Worthy
- Regretful, Remorseful, Sorry
- Relieved, Satisfied
- Selfish, Ungenerous
- Self-satisfied, Smug
- Sensitive, Touchy
- Shy, Timid
- Suspicious

- Touched
- Triggered
- Unsafe, Vulnerable
- Vengeful
- Withdrawn

You might notice that I haven't included "good' or "bad' as feelings. They are just too vague. Let's go back for a minute to the petting zoo, where you and your toddler see a duck, a chicken, and a goose. You probably wouldn't identify each of them as "bird" — it only makes sense to be as specific as possible. Likewise, your son doesn't just feel bad; he feels angry, frustrated, scared, worried, annoyed, indignant, ashamed, or some other unpleasant emotion. When you can see that your daughter feels good, is it because she is feeling brave? Proud? Surprised? Loved? Excited? Joyful?

We can use rich emotional language when our kids are behaving well. Parents often rely on a thin repertoire of reactions to desired behavior — "Yay! Good boy!" or "You're being so *nice!*" or "That's my big girl!" Try using livelier words to describe precisely what's good about a behavior:

- "Thank you! It was so *helpful* of you to bring me a clean diaper for Joshua."
- "That was really *friendly* of you to let him use the puzzle!"
- "What a *thoughtful* thing you did! Look how she's smiling!"

Instead of validating kids for being "nice" with bland, vague responses, we can teach them in specific terms what's good about "being good." These cues help them draw their own conclusions about sociability, as in the examples above:

- *People feel grateful when I do favors for them.*
- *When I share, it makes other kids want to be my friend.*
- *I can figure out what someone else wants and make him/her happy by providing it.*

It's important to use emotion-words accurately. How often grownups say things like "you're a little upset" when in fact the child is enraged! This discounts the depth and intensity of her feeling-state and says more about how we are responding emotionally than about what she is experiencing. We wish to dial down the emotion, so we call it something it isn't. Not only is this ineffectual, but it's like telling her that bright turquoise is baby blue. Dishonesty is confusing.

We should also use the words respectfully. "Oh, you're just jealous!" (said teasingly or scornfully) doesn't offer insight. It's a put-down. Feeling jealous is a painful experience, one that gnaws at a person's insides. Anyone who is feeling envy is uncomfortable enough, and the last thing he needs is to feel ashamed of that feeling.

"Don't be mad" and "Don't be sad" are other things we sometimes say that are out of sync with the feeling someone is having. The words are meant to console, but what we are actually doing is telegraphing our own discomfort with strong negative emotion and denying the other person's right to feel what he feels. We may have to help a child channel a potentially destructive impulse — anger, for example — but our effort will be more successful if we support rather than deny the core feeling.

It takes courage to accept a distressed person's emotion with empathy and without trying to change or fix the feeling. Dwelling in a negative emotion is one of the greatest gifts we can give to another person, especially a child. Our calm, empathetic acceptance of what she is experiencing reassures her that the feeling will pass and that she doesn't need to be rescued with distraction or false cheer. When distress is met with calm empathy, kids learn that unpleasant feelings are survivable.

In addition to building self-awareness and a comfortable familiarity with feeling-states, emotion words act as bridges to empathy. Young children are naturally self-centered, and it's difficult for them to draw connections to what others are feeling. Let's say that a few days ago Anthony was leaving the ice cream store with his dad. Just as they stepped off the curb, Anthony's ice cream toppled to the ground. Devastated, Anthony began to cry. His dad bent down and hugged him. "Oh, Anthony, you were so excited and happy about the cone, and then it fell! You look *so disappointed!*" (In this particular situation, it was possible to replace the cone, whereas of course sometimes we can only help by dwelling with a child in a disappointment that simply has to be endured.)

Today, Anthony is at preschool. It's time to go home, and he notices his friend Jacob sobbing by the gate. Their teacher is hugging Jacob and patting his back. Anthony sidles over to see what's up. (Is he moved by empathy or just curiosity? Who can say?) The teacher says, "Anthony, it's so friendly of you to come and see how Jacob is doing. Would you like to know why he's crying?" (Anthony nods solemnly.) She explains, "Jacob had a plan to go play at his cousin's house. Remember? He talked about it at circle time and made a picture of his cousin at the art table this afternoon. He was really anticipating a fun play date with him. We just got a call that his cousin came down with a cold, so Jacob's mother is going to pick him up and take him home instead. Jacob's feeling *very disappointed.*"

"Disappointed" — bingo! *Jacob must be feeling what I felt.* The similarity between a wrecked ice cream cone and a canceled play date is very abstract concept for a preschooler, but the word "disappointed" — and all the poignancy the word evokes for Anthony — is a bridge of empathy that helps him to connect with Jacob's experience. Anthony's father could not possibly have predicted that his son would have the opportunity to relate to another child's disappointment in the days immediately following the ice cream incident. But he began construction on that bridge anyway. Luckily, another empathetic adult was there waiting on the other side.

## I-MESSAGES

I think of I-messages and active listening as the meat and potatoes of good communication. We are indebted to clinical psychologist Thomas Gordon for coining the term "I-message" in the 1960s. He went on to develop the concept in a book for parents, *P.E.T.: Parent Effectiveness Training.* Gordon's purpose was to maximize the speaker's impact while minimizing the listener's defensiveness. I-messages are surprisingly contagious. The more you model I-messages, the more you'll hear the people around you using them.

An I-message is deceptively simple to construct. It goes like this: *I feel [emotion] when you [action]*:

- I feel *discouraged* when you *walk out on a discussion*
- I get *grouchy* when you *leave crusty dishes in the sink*
- I feel so *contented* when you *cuddle with me after dinner*

The important elements of an I-message are *my feeling* and *your behavior*. I-messages work their magic in a lot of ways. To begin with, they enrich communication. When you are bothered by someone else's behavior, an I-message gets the idea across without accusing or humiliating that person. You are simply giving them information about the impact of their action on your feeling-state. You are providing that person with the opportunity to make an important choice. What I find especially powerful about I-messages is that they can't be refuted. They are basically inarguable. You are talking about a feeling that is owned by you. No one is likely to counter with "No, you don't feel like that."

Remember to use I-messages when you are pleased as well as displeased! When you are happy with someone's behavior, giving an I-message allows you to be very specific about what you liked and how it made you feel. An I-message is a wonderful way to validate desired behavior. Consider how much richer it is to say to a child, "I felt so relaxed and happy at the restaurant because you stayed in your seat. Thank you!" than a stock comment like "good boy."

When people forget to use an I-message, it invites defensiveness and leaves room for changing the subject:

Mom: You are so lazy! You never put your socks in the hamper!

Son: That's not true! Last week after practice, I put my muddy
socks right in there!

Suddenly they are talking about whether the son has *ever* put his
socks in the hamper. By using the word "never," Mom has made an
exaggerated, categorical accusation that her son finds easy to knock
down. However, the fact that he may have put his socks in the
hamper a week ago Thursday is quite beside the point that Mom
wants to get across: how she feels when he doesn't do it — which is
most of the time. He gets it that she is mad. Mom gets mad a lot. But
he doesn't know exactly how she feels because, in truth, she hasn't
told him. And he's not positioned to own his role in causing this
feeling.

Of course, Mom got off to a bad start in a number of ways. She
put her son down by calling him a disrespectful name. And the first
word out of her mouth was "you." When people see an angry look
on your face and hear the word "you," they brace for the defense —
as well they might! The son was poised to deflect Mom's accusation
even before all the words were out of her mouth. Let's see how Mom
could have gotten her point across as an I-message:

Mom: I feel so frustrated and disrespected when I see dirty
socks lying next to the hamper!

Son: (surprised) Oh! ... um ... yeah ...

I-messages can be disarming. The son is nearly speechless. He
hasn't exactly said, "O Mother Dear, I swear to mend my evil ways,"
but by the same token he is not busy playing defense. He is free to
think things over. Without judging or criticizing, his mother has
given him some very useful information about how his behavior
affects her state of mind. She lets it sink in. Perhaps there is an
awkward silence — fine! — before she speaks again.

Mom: Do you think you could help me solve this problem?

Son: I guess ... yeah, OK.

Mom: What will that look like?

Son: Well ... I'll put them in the hamper.

Mom: Thanks!

It needn't end there. If the son is compliant for a couple of days, she can say, "I appreciate how you really listened to me about the socks. It makes such a difference in how I feel when I go in your room to collect the laundry. Thanks again!"

The easiest way to teach children to use I-messages is to model them. However, very young children (or older kids who are new at it) might find it easier if you address the action and the feeling about that action separately. By breaking up the I-message into its two component parts, you can simplify the process and get more clarity:

- What did he do that bothered you? ("He won't share the truck.")
- And how did that make you feel? ("Mad")
- Can you tell him those two things together? ("It makes me mad when you don't share the truck.")

It will come as no surprise that I-messages also work well with spouses, friends, neighbors, and co-workers. If I-messages are new to you, the same process will work for you that works for kids in framing one. First, try to catch yourself when you begin a sentence with "you" — or even worse, "you always ... " or "you never ... " Then ask yourself, *what am I feeling and what was the trigger?* Take a deep breath. Deliver that I-message.

## ACTIVE LISTENING

Like "I-message," the term "active listening" was popularized by Dr. Thomas Gordon. According to Gordon Training International, its creator was Dr. Carl Rogers, who called it "reflective listening." The term "active listening" was coined by Richard Farson, and then introduced to the world by Dr. Gordon.

Active listening is simple — but it's not easy. Like the I-message, it's a learned behavior, and it can become a habit. If you model it, kids will follow your lead. It's a way of drawing someone out, helping her process feelings that are compelling but not understood by her — emotions that may still be nameless. You sometimes have to start with something vague ("You look really down"), and gradually work your way toward something specific as you get more information. ("It must have been so discouraging for you when he said that.") Like an I-message, active listening can contain an emotion *and* a situation (or trigger). In this sense, it's like an inverted I-message:

- "It sounds like you get really annoyed when he hums."
- "What I'm hearing is that you feel disrespected when she calls you Shorty."
- "You looked absolutely thrilled when he invited you to play catch."

For ideas about how to begin, have a look at the active listening "openers" found later in this chapter.

Sometimes the hardest time to use active listening is when it's most needed. When your teenager comes home and angrily yells, "Mr. Henderson sucks!" You're not exactly going to be feeling all warm and fuzzy. You experience a knee-jerk reaction to the crude language and the sweeping grandiosity. You might give in to the temptation to launch into a lecture about respecting one's elders or Mr. Henderson's sterling reputation as a calculus teacher or how offended you are by ugly speech. Or all three. And — you knew this even before you began to speak — your dissertation will be met with a slammed door.

But who slammed the first door? After all, *your kid began the conversation*. Granted, it was quite an opener. It was raw and offensive, a verbal shard hurled by an adolescent who is struggling with self-regulation. But he could have just walked in the door, withheld his anger, and taken it to his room. Instead, he shared it (in his clumsy and unreflective way) with *you*. This was an invitation, of sorts, for you to help him process all that he's feeling. Now he's holed up in his room, angrier than ever. You're baffled and worried. Something bad happened at school, and you have absolutely no idea what it was. Without meaning to at all, you have foreclosed on two critically important opportunities: getting more information, and helping your kid understand and manage a bad situation.

Lecturing instead of using active listening is pretty much like slamming the first door. In *Your Child's Self-Esteem*, a terrific and much-misinterpreted book (see Annotated Bibliography) Dorothy Corkille Briggs wrote, "When you share personal feelings, you don't want judgment, logic, reasons, or advice. You don't want your feelings brushed aside, denied, or taken lightly." She called this class of responses "feeling stoppers." They look like this (the examples in quotes are mine):

- Cheering: "Don't worry — you always do well on history tests!"
- Reasoning: "Kicking the block tower just makes *all* the blocks fall. If you want a high tower, just keep trying and don't get angry."
- Judgment: "That's a terrible thing to say about your brother. You're supposed to love each other!"
- Denial: "There's nothing to be afraid of."

Each of these dismisses the child's feeling. Active listening responses might look something like this:

- "It's odd ... you usually do really well on history tests, but for some reason you're really worried about this one. I wonder why ... "
- "You want to build a huge, tall tower! It feels so frustrating when you work hard and some of the blocks fall. You got

so mad you kicked all of them down ... and now you're
feeling disappointed."
- "What I'm hearing is that you are really, really angry at La
  Shawn. Do you want to talk to him about that?"
- "Sounds like you're afraid there's a monster under the bed.
  How can I help you not feel so scared?"

Active listening is not only useful in helping your child
understand and manage strong feelings. It's also a wonderful
technique to deploy when your child wants something she can't
have. It's almost counter-intuitive: your preschooler is asking for a
cookie at 5 PM, and the answer is "no." So why would you want to
admit that cookies are delicious and that it would be fun to have one
right now? Doesn't that undermine discipline? Actually, no — it can
serve to soften the blow and help a child feel less belligerent. To a
small child, "feeling felt" is nearly as important as getting her way.
Even very young children know when you are being inauthentic,
and they find it infuriating: "Oh, you don't want a cookie *now*. It's
almost dinnertime!" Kids warm to the emotional truth, and this
usually engages more cooperation: "You really love those yummy
chocolate chip cookies! I do too! I wish I could have one right now.
But we have to wait until after dinner to enjoy one ... it's hard to
wait, I know."

Active listening works by engaging. It draws someone closer and
invites the person to confide. Using empathy and intuition, we're
able to make inferences about someone else's emotional state.
Especially when we know a person really well, we can make a pretty
good guess how they are feeling. In that sense, active listening
(though far from being an exact science) is evidence-based. We
interpret the *words we hear* and the *body language we observe*. If we're
not on solid ground, we can actively listen in vague terms, which
invites self-reflection and allows for some tweaking:

Q: "Sounds like Mr. Henderson did something that *really*
upset you. Are you feeling angry?"

A: "Not really ... I guess ... I guess I'm more frustrated than anything."

Active listening should feel tentative. The probing works best when done gently and respectfully. It's just a way of asking to be invited in.

## FIFTEEN WAYS TO SAY "I'M LISTENING"

1. "In other words, you ..."
2. "So, to be clear [to clarify] ..."
3. "So, long story short ..."
4. "I want to be sure I've heard [understood] what you said ..."
5. "Let me see if I got this right ..."
6. "Then I think what you're saying is ... "
7. "Are you saying that ... ?"
8. "Tell me if this sounds right ..."
9. "Help me understand ..."
10. "It sounds like you ..."
11. "What I'm hearing is ..."
12. "If I heard [understood] you correctly ..."
13. "So, my understanding is ..."
14. "It sounds [seems] like you're saying ..."
15. "To summarize ..."

## ATTRIBUTION — BEWARE!

Side-by-side with active listening, I want to mention its evil twin, a thing mediators call "attribution." Attribution is the tendency we all have to imagine (and then believe) that we know why someone else did or said something. It's like empathy gone amok! It's great to try to get in someone else's head in order to help them process their feelings, as with active listening. We can use our powers of observation and our empathy to notice other people's emotion states, and to respond warmly by making inferences about how they are feeling. Sometimes we can even guess what may have been the trigger. Active Listening seeks to *understand*. Attribution, on the other hand, seeks to *blame*. It usually gets called into play when someone threatens or angers us. We "otherize" an opponent by casting him or her in the worst possible light. We invent an evil motive and then use it as evidence:

- "She told me not to wear my cute blue sweater because she didn't want Justin to notice me."
- "He broke the date to study together because he wanted to get a better grade than me!"
- "You're not letting me go to the party because you didn't have any fun when you were a teenager, and you don't want me to, either!"

It's no wonder that when we make an attribution to someone's face (as in the last outburst above, in which a teenage girl attacks her mother's position about going to a party) we invite pushback. Attribution is presumptuous and maddening. (*How can you possibly know why I did something when half the time I don't even know myself?*) Attribution is pseudo-insight, driven by a desire to discredit someone. The teenager's attribution has put her mother on the defensive, and Mom will probably respond by elaborating on her actual reason (the safety of her daughter) in terms that are inflated, self-promoting and repetitive. This will further aggravate the situation.

When did the daughter learn attribution? Little kids are prone to this type of thinking, probably because of a combination of things: having lively imaginations, engaging in magical thinking, and being egocentric. A preschooler finds it easy to invent motives, she thinks she's a bit of a mind-reader, and she's self-centered enough to believe that anyone whose needs run counter to hers is just plain mean. However, we meet lots of adults who have not outgrown attribution. As a mediator, I see how it initiates fresh conflicts as well as aggravates existing ones. People find it both infuriating and exasperating. Attribution is a habit of mind, and a bad one. It's reinforced when kids hear it from those around them. The best prevention, of course, is for parents to avoid this kind of talk.

But how to react when our kids do it? The best antidote for attribution that I have come across is The Rule of Six. I was introduced to this technique by Michelle Seely, a licensed marriage and family therapist, who learned it from teacher Shari Majumder. Shari learned it from Paula Underwood (Turtle Woman Singing) who learned it from her Oneida great-grandmother. The Rule of Six holds that there can be multiple explanations for any phenomenon, action, or utterance. Michelle came up with the idea of using the upheld hand to illustrate the rule. The palm represents the situation and the five fingers and arm radiating from the palm represent six different explanations or interpretations. The arm, being largest and most obvious, can represent the original assumption made — what Michelle calls "worst first." This might be the attribution we make out of fear, suspicion, envy, or anger.

Suppose your kindergartener, Hannah, says "Jeremy wouldn't let me play blocks with him because he doesn't like girls." She may be quite fixed on this belief. Hurt and insulted, she has convinced herself that it is so. Using Hannah's own upheld arm to diagram the situation, inscribe the behavior in her palm: *Jeremy wouldn't play blocks with me*. The wrist and forearm, being strong and thick, represent her attribution — the worst-first reason Hannah's mind seized upon: *Jeremy doesn't like girls*. Using each of her outspread fingers, brainstorm with Hannah other possible reasons for Jeremy's behavior. Take your time. Encourage her to use that great imagination that came up with the attribution in the first place. Try to get her to do the heavy lifting, but you can throw in a reason or two of your own until you have labeled all five fingers:

1. Maybe Jeremy was just feeling grouchy and needed some alone-time ... or
2. Maybe he just didn't want to share ideas with another kid in building the tower ... or

3. Maybe he was still mad that Hannah called him a mean name last week ... or

4. Maybe he thought there weren't enough blocks for two people to enjoy together ... or

5. Maybe he was in a hurry to finish the tower before cleanup time

Or maybe, or maybe, or maybe. It's a game, one that widens a person's outlook. Now we have six possible reasons instead of just one. Perspective-taking has been called into play. Once Hannah has played The Rule of Six about Jeremy and the blocks, her thinking has been dislodged from the original attribution. Note that the object of the exercise is not to replace one attribution with another; the challenge is to hold more than one idea at a time. This mental exercise is both disciplined and humbling: *there are multiple possibilities, and we can't know which is correct.* If Hannah's mom or dad had sat her down and presented "all the maybes" in lecture form, Hannah wouldn't have processed the experience in the same way, and it wouldn't have had the same impact. By rummaging around in her own imagination to come up with a number of possible explanations for Jeremy's behavior, Hannah has taught herself, in effect, that attribution is a sketchy and unreliable thing.

There's a world of difference between "When you said that, you looked like you were maybe feeling a little jealous" (active listening, which addresses evident emotion) and "You just said that because you wanted to get him in trouble" (attribution, which addresses motive.) Intentions are hidden from sight, so we can't really know for sure what motivates another person. As we saw in the previous section, active listening invites *engagement.* Attribution is a conversational dead-end because it yields the opposite result — *disengagement.*

### Insisting on Reframes of Insulting Language

Insults and put-downs are staples of sibling conflict. As parents, we have choices about how to react. If we let insults slide, they become like the ugly wallpaper in a new apartment. Leave the wallpaper up, and pretty soon you no longer wince when you see it. It becomes an accepted part of your environment. After a while, the dispiriting effect of that ugly wallpaper stops being conscious. But in a subliminal way, it will continue to bring everybody down.

The problem with letting insults slide is not just that they contribute a mild toxicity to the atmosphere of your home. And it's not just that tolerance of put-downs allows them to become ingrained and habitual. What's especially unfortunate about letting a put-down slide is that this is a missed opportunity for some real communication. When a preschooler calls his sister a "poopy-head," he's trying to *say something*. Maybe he's angry, and he would like his sister to change her behavior. When you help him reframe his insult into an I-message, he not only gets to develop and refine what's on his mind — he might actually get results!

In Chapter Three, Section 3, we saw how Helen helped Alex reframe his insult to baby brother Amos. Helen started with some active listening and invited Alex to present Amos with an I-message. I called this a "Mediation in Miniature" because Helen tailored her efforts to the very young age and short attention span of the participants. It wasn't a full-fledged mediation because Amos doesn't yet have the words (or the self-control, for that matter) to agree to change his behavior. But because his mom took the time to help his big brother reframe an insult into an I-message, the toddler has some interesting information to mull over: *My brother was embarrassed by my behavior.* At the same time, Helen accomplished another goal: to discourage insulting language in her home by nipping it in the bud. She did this not by shutting Alex down or scolding him for being "mean" or telling him to "be nice" but by redirecting his message by means of a reframe.

I presented the mechanics of inviting reframes in Chapter Six under "Rely on Reframes." We saw how very young children may need help breaking down their experience into a feeling and a trigger before they can deliver the message re-packaged as an I-message. This begins with some active listening and continues with a probing question or two about how the child is feeling and what behavior prompted that feeling. It concludes with an invitation to deliver an I-message. (It sounds complicated, but this whole thing shouldn't take more than thirty seconds.) Older kids, experienced communicators who have temporarily fallen off the I-message wagon, will respond to a shorthand cue such as "Re-do, please!" or "Hey, Tyler — let's have a reframe!"

We know that reframing works to extinguish other annoying behaviors. Whining, for example, is something that drives parents crazy, and the best cure is a simple one. Each and every time your child whines you respond with "Please say that in your regular voice" or "Can you ask that again in your regular voice?" You may have to do this 25, 50, 75 times — but your determined, consistent refusal to give in to whining will eventually do the trick because no child wants to go to the trouble of saying everything twice. There's an economy of expression that governs how all of us communicate: *Why should I say A and then B when I know that it's B that's going to get me what I want?*

It works the same with insults. If you consistently and calmly invite your child to transform every put-down into an I-message, it soon becomes a bother to hurl insults. The oftener you insist on a reframe, and the more determined you are not to let insults slide, the less inclined your children will be to make statements that are out of bounds, and the better they will get at delivering I-messages the first time around. And, as I've said before, I-messages tend to serve as their own reward because they are so effective in bringing about desired results. This process is easiest if (like Helen) you nip insulting behavior in the bud as soon as your kids become verbal. However, if you are patient and persistent, it can be accomplished with kids of any age. Letting insults slide is a habit, one that can be replaced with the habit of using I-messages.

As a mom, I found that the most challenging reframes happened not when one of my children verbally attacked the other, but when my child insulted *me*. Sooner or later most young kids (infuriated because you have laid down the law about this or that) will initiate what to me is the Mother of All Reframes: "I hate you! You're a bad mommy!" This cuts to the quick, and it's particularly devastating to hear if we have angry or conflicted feelings about our own parents. Even for those of us who have pretty healthy feelings about our folks, it's never fun to hear this. It's understandable why a lot of parents react to this challenge by lashing out, or furiously defending themselves, or relenting. And yet we know that attack, defend, and cave-in are all reactions that can take the situation to an even worse place.

So how to react to this emotional body-blow? First of all, *breathe*. Know that young kids don't get the difference between hate and anger. In the moment (which is precisely where they live), their passionate anger *feels* to them like hate. And they blurt out their feelings, completely unprocessed.

Try active listening: "Wow, it sounds like you are really furious at me right now. Sometimes we get really, *really* angry at people we love. Would you like to tell me how mad you are?" At this point, your child may refuse, stomping out with an unrepentant "No! You're a mean mommy and I hate you." Don't follow or continue to engage. You cannot win this one. You've thrown a few seeds in the soil. Who knows, maybe they'll take root.

Or your child might accept the invitation and holler "I'm so mad" or "I'm angry that you have that dumb rule about cookies before dinner." Briefly validate: "Thank you for telling me how you feel" or "I see that that rule makes you very, *very* angry." And — you're done. At this point, please don't give in to the impulse to deliver a nutritional lecture in order to defend your position or soften your child's position. Strong emotion trumps rational discourse every time. Know that you have the responsibility of setting limits and that it's natural for your child to chafe at them even as he struggles to stay within bounds. You invited him to express a powerful feeling. He has reframed an ugly and hurtful insult into a strong I-message. Now just let him feel entitled to his emotion.

Later, when everyone has calmed down, you might want to issue an I-message of your own: "You know, yesterday when you said I'm a mean mommy and you hate me, I felt sad and insulted. When you said it differently — when you talked about the cookie rule and how angry you were — I felt much better. And it was easier for me to understand

how you felt." You have a right to get this off your chest, and your
child has a right to know how his behavior impacts *your* emotion
states. Today, after everyone has had a chance to cool off, your message
stands a chance of sinking in. You would have been wasting your
breath to say it yesterday, when your child was flooded — and
therefore blocked to incoming information — with his own feelings.

Reframes are empowering. They help kids develop the ability to
communicate their feelings authentically, acceptably, and effectively.
Even red-hot anger and ice-cold resentment can be understood and
regulated through the use of the reframe. In this way, reframing acts
as an emotional thermostat for the family, giving parents the power
to maintain a household climate of respect and relative harmony.

### STEERING CLEAR OF SHAME

Imagine that you're in the car on your way to work with your
kids in the back seat. It's been a crazy-hectic morning, and a glance at
the clock tells you that the kids are going to be marked tardy, and
that you're going to be late for work as well. Feeling pressured and
aggravated, you run a red light. There is a terrible screech of brakes
from a car you didn't see coming from your left; you brake too, and
the other car misses yours by mere inches. You can see that the other
driver has a child in the back seat. He opens his car door and yells,
"You stupid &$%$#!! What do you think you're doing? Better learn
to drive before you get someone killed!" With that, he slams the
door, backs up sharply, and takes off.

Flushed with anger, your heart racing, you take off for work.
Random thoughts tumble frantically through your mind:

- *What a jerk, using awful language like that around kids!*
- *How embarrassing it would be if any of my friends or neighbors
  witnessed that verbal flogging!*
- *People who drive that kind of car always think they are better
  than everyone else!*
- *He had a lot of nerve, frightening me and my children like that!*

Your children are cowering in fear, but one of them gathers the nerve to pipe up and ask what happened. You answer, "Oh, he's just some jerk who thinks he owns the road. There was nothing to get excited about. We didn't even crash! Decent people don't talk like that. What a horrible man!"

Now let's look at the same scenario with a different outcome.

You're in the car on your way to work, with your kids in the back seat. It's been a crazy-hectic morning, and a glance at the clock tells you that the kids are going to be marked tardy and that you're going to be late for work as well. Feeling pressured and aggravated, you run a red light. There is a terrible screech of brakes from a car you didn't see coming from your left; you brake too, and the other car misses yours by mere inches. You can see that the other driver has a child in the back seat. He quickly checks the back to make sure his child is OK. Turning forward, he grips the wheel and takes a couple of deep breaths to steady himself. He makes eye contact with you and acknowledges the look of fear and horror on your face. Backing up, he leaves the scene.

Your heart racing, you pull over to the side of the road. Your thoughts tumble:

- *We were incredibly lucky our cars didn't crash.*
- *I'm so grateful no one got hurt.*
- *That was a really stupid risk I took.*
- *By taking a foolish chance, I made us even later.*
- *Nothing is worth endangering my kids' lives or the lives of others.*
- *From now on, I'm going to try really hard not to let my emotional state affect my driving.*

Your children are cowering in fear, but one of them gathers the nerve to pipe up and ask what happened. You answer, "I was worried about being late, and I did something I shouldn't have. I took a terrible chance when I ran that red light. We're very lucky no one got hurt. I'm going to do everything I can to drive more carefully from now on." Checking the rear view mirror, you ease out into the rush hour traffic.

What's different about the two scenarios is the difference between shame and remorse. I think of shame as outside-in and remorse as inside-out. When we are shamed, a negative outside force throws all our mind's resources into defense mode, causing us to furiously seek ways to justify ourselves and discredit the shamer. When shame isn't brought into play, and we are left to our own devices after wrongdoing, our thinking is much freer. We experience an interior sense of discomfort with what we've done, and we want to act on it. We are able to *reflect* (ponder what we did and why it was a bad idea) and *resolve* (make a decision to change our behavior.) That, to me, is what remorse is all about.

Shame is a lousy teacher because it changes the subject. We usually know when we have done something wrong. But if someone humiliates us about our wrongdoing, all the mental energy that should be put toward reflecting/resolving gets deployed defending a wounded ego. Shame directs us toward vengeance instead of self-awareness. It strangles remorse, robbing us of the ability to do that all-important work: to think about what we did and set an intention to change. This has tremendous implications for how we teach our children right from wrong.

Little kids don't always know when they have done something wrong. How can we teach them while leaving shame out of the equation — so they can really learn? And by *learn*, I mean develop an understanding that will motivate them to discontinue or modify the misbehavior. What toddlers and preschoolers need, above all, is *information*:

"I think she's crying because the mask you were wearing scared her."

"Next time, please put newspaper down first so paint doesn't get on the kitchen table."

"Pinching hurts his body. When you hurt him, it makes him not want to play with you."

Parents are often dismayed to learn that genuine remorse doesn't usually kick in for quite a while. It evolves alongside empathy, and we usually don't see active signs of it until the ages of about three to five. Once the child experiences remorse, you have something to work with — but it still requires a delicate touch. A child might withdraw after he does something wrong, looking sad or out of sorts. Gentle probing might help the child identify what happened, how he's feeling about it, and how he might follow up. You may be able to steer him toward making amends (more about restitution later in this chapter, under "Apologies.") At this stage of life, most kids are amenable to doing some reflecting/resolving out loud, with the parent as coach.

School-age kids and teenagers still sometimes need coaching in order to process wrongdoing. Their awareness of right and wrong might be well developed, but self-control lags behind any code of good behavior that they have absorbed. Careful reading of body language paired with gentle questions can help:

- "You looked really down after Jared went home. Do you want to talk about it?"
- "What were your clues that she was upset with you?"
- "If something like that happened again, how do you think you could handle it differently?"

And what about shaming lite? Even something as seemingly innocuous as saying "I told you so" has an edge to it that is counterproductive. Let's say the weather forecast predicts afternoon rain, and you have to talk your fifth-grader into letting you stuff a rainproof jacket in his backpack. Later, he returns from school in the pouring rain, wearing the jacket. Can you resist the temptation to say "I told you so?" Can you? To begin with, *he knows perfectly well you told him so*. It's immature and petty for a parent to crow about this kind of "victory." And it distracts the child from the lesson by inviting him to focus on how self-righteous and annoying the parent is. Let him be. That way, you allow what's important to sink in:

*Getting a weather forecast isn't a bad idea.*

*I'm sure glad I didn't get soaking wet.*

*Dad really knew what he was talking about!*

Not saying "I told you so" increases the odds that your child will have a useful "live and learn" experience — as well as a positive association connecting you to the good counsel you provided. After all, it's critically important that your child build and maintain an image of you as a reliable source of information and advice.

Sad to say, shame has been a time-honored way of shutting down behaviors parents don't like. It can be hard to resist shaming a child who has behaved badly. After all, it's a convenient shortcut. However, it doesn't build character because it prevents deeper learning by derailing the reflecting/resolving process. Shame also demeans the spirit and erodes the parent-child relationship.

This poses a huge challenge to the parent who grew up in a household where shame was used as a weapon to control and modify children's behavior. It requires deep intention for this parent not to shame his own children when they misbehave or otherwise disappoint him. Fortunately, there are more positive and character-building ways of teaching good behavior. Some family traditions should be put to rest. Shaming talk is a bad habit that deserves to be broken.

## Is Sharing a "Should"?

Whenever toddlers and preschoolers play together, whether at school or day care, play dates or birthday parties, the issue of sharing always arises. As adults, we have funny ideas about sharing. I have seen parents insist that a child hand something over to another child and then praise him for sharing. To me, that's not sharing — it's a shakedown.

When we say "sharing," I think we mean two distinct things. First there's sharing in the sense of the generous impulse. A child notices that another child is deprived in some way, feels bad about that, and seeks to address the need: perhaps he sees another child sadly eying his cookie and divides it in half so they can both have some.

Then there is the process definition. This sense of sharing is a whole problem-solving event starting with the recognition that two kids want the same toy and followed by some negotiating. The outcome might involve working out a way to use the toy together or deciding to take turns. Both aspects of sharing — having generous impulses as well as knowing how to problem-solve — are complicated. They each require some maturity, self-control, and empathy. Sharing, in the process sense of the word, can be addressed through mediation. Children learn to problem-solve in a relatively calm state of mind with the goal of compromising on a solution.

Here I want to talk more in depth about sharing in the sense of the generous impulse. Sharing resources is probably the commonest challenge to siblings and the biggest source of sibling conflict. As parents, we want to raise kids who aren't grabby, who know how to take turns, and who recognize the rights of others. The tricky thing is that we must start monitoring children's social behavior when they are still socially immature and self-centered, long before they have developed much real empathy.

This is not to say that very young children, even babies, are completely oblivious to the feelings of others. Research has shown that babies take note of other babies in distress, and that even in the first year of life children recognize, and show a marked preference for, kindness and altruism. But in everyday play situations, babies and toddlers have very much a "me first" approach to things. To me, the tiny bit of empathy we're born with is a small and fragile ember that needs constant fanning, as well as protection from the wind and rain, in order for it to turn into a fire big enough to provide warmth. We begin fanning that flame with babies:

"You're noticing that Teesha is crying. I wonder what's bothering her? "

"This banana is so yummy I want to share it with you!"

"Oh, look — Jordan brought you the book. That was so friendly!"

It can seem like a very long wait until one's toddler or preschooler spontaneously hands over a toy or shares a piece of her cookie with another child. At last, she experiences that magical impulse to be generous. She does something kind, without prompting and purely out of the goodness of her heart. It feels like a tiny miracle. This is a moment worth waiting for! Your child has put a big smile on another child's face. That, along with your warm, pleased reaction, sets in motion the habit of a lifetime — generosity. How sad it would be for your child (or you, her parent) to be deprived of such a moment.

I worry that a lot of forced sharing can do just that, by short-circuiting the process. Forcing a child to share robs the child of the opportunity to find generosity on the inside, where it is pleasurable and meaningful. This is especially true with siblings. Parents often have unrealistic expectations of an older sibling, even when the two children are very young and close in age. When we insist that one child give up a toy because the other child is smaller, younger, weaker, etc., we take a bad idea ("might makes right") and turn it on its head to produce another bad idea. If a toddler or young preschooler who happens to be a big sister is always expected to be the giver-upper, she may never get to experience that magical impulse from within. Rather than bringing joy, sharing brings feelings of deprivation and resentment. Generosity (or whatever passes for generosity) is always a chore, never a delight.

I really like the way Samuel (Chapter Three, Section 6, "The Young and the Restless") handled the dispute between Luis and Marisela. He recognized that, at ages three and one-and-a-half, they are simply two very young kids with a problem: what happens when they both want the same truck. Samuel didn't impose any *shoulds* upon his son just because Luis is the older child. And he certainly didn't drag in any nonsense about how "gentlemen" behave toward "ladies." Patience and empathy-building will allow Luis' fellow-feeling and generosity to flower in their own good time. Meanwhile, disputes about who has what can be addressed in a matter-of-fact way through mediation, a process made fair by power-balancing. Samuel uses mediation as a tool for filling that huge gap between "Mine!" and "Would you like half of my cookie?"

I also worry that forced sharing interferes with the development of self-control. In a way this is counter-intuitive, because doesn't it take a lot of self-control for the older child to relinquish something? Yes and no. This kind of bogus sharing will happen when the parent is hovering, and it will probably not happen when the parent isn't nearby.

For a behavior to become an ingrained habit, there has to be some incentive — and continual deprivation is hardly a strong motivator! To be gratifying, self-control should make way for some kind of process that feels fair and produces reasonably satisfactory results for the child struggling to master his impulses. Let's imagine that Samuel always insists that Luis share with Marisela because she's the baby, much younger than Luis, "and a girl besides." How would Luis describe this situation, if he could?

> *Self-control doesn't produce good results for me. The way things are, when I control myself I experience loss, and I feel like a pushover. A generous person is a loser. If my only choice is to relinquish or be the victor, I will learn to be grabby and not to make a place for fairness. Since self-control doesn't work in my favor, I'll just be sneaky and snatch stuff because I can — on account of my age, size, speed, and ability to intimidate.*

Genuine sharing takes a long time to kick in, but it's worth waiting for. Just like genuine remorse, the impulse to share springs from empathy. We can set the stage by fanning that tiny flame of empathy, however elusive and flickering. In the meantime, taking each dispute on a case-by-case basis, rather than imposing counterfeit sharing on our kids, will allow true generosity of spirit to emerge and flourish.


### Apologies and Forgiveness

When was the last time you heard a spontaneous, heartfelt, unqualified apology? We sure hear a lot of fake apologies, don't we? Consider the difference between the following pairs of statements:

"I'm sorry I'm late but ... [litany of excuses]"
"My lateness must have been an inconvenience to you. I'm so sorry."

"Mistakes were made."
"I made mistakes."

"I'm sorry if I hurt your feelings."
"I'm sorry I hurt your feelings."

It's not hard to spot the difference between the fake apologies and the real ones. Grownups often force children to apologize, and yet we have so much trouble doing it ourselves! I suspect there's a connection. Forced apologies are often fused with humiliation: "You should be ashamed of yourself! You go right over there, and apologize to her!" The result of this is that the child feels sorry indeed, but only because apologizing brings embarrassment upon him, and not for the desired, higher-level reason — empathy for the child he wronged and a desire to make things right. Kids gradually come to associate apologizing with feeling shamed and cornered. It's a penalty, one that makes them feel less than, diminished, and resentful. No wonder that when they become adults, they become expert at issuing the evasive "fauxpology." (Hats off to the blogger by the name of Gregoire who coined this clever term in 2005!)

So what can we do to nurture empathy, ownership of wrongdoing, and the desire to make things right? You guessed it ...

we can *wait*. Just as we can wait for generosity to kick in (as in the previous section of this chapter) we can wait for remorse. This is hard to do, but if you treat your child with respect and empathy, and if you use a lot of emotion-words to describe her feeling states and the emotions of those around her, she will eventually get it. In the meantime, it's perfectly all right to say *you* are sorry if your child is in the wrong. Suppose your toddler Alison hits her friend Lucia. You could say something like "Lucia, I'm sorry Alison hit you. That must have really hurt." And to your toddler, "Alison, Lucia is crying because it really hurts her body when you hit her. It looks to me like she's feeling sad and angry." Not only is this good modeling, but it's also authentic. After all, Alison is the person you're responsible for socializing, and you probably do feel bad that she hit Lucia.

Sooner or later your child will be ready for some gentle coaching. I will never forget watching my good friend Christine Colton doing this with her kids and the other children in her care. We were in our early twenties and Chris, a young mom, was running a family day care home. Not yet a parent myself, I observed in amazement as she coached a four-year-old child who had hurt one of the others. Instead of indignation or judgment, what she offered was empathy, insight, and some gentle prodding. She was helping him understand that the "funny feeling" in his stomach was remorse. And she helped him decide what to do about it, which relieved him as well as the child he'd hurt.

I learned from watching Chris that a good indication of coaching-readiness is that the wrongdoer appears glum or even grouchy, as though under a cloud. In the case above, let's say that Alison and Lucia are now preschoolers. Alison has hit Lucia and then withdrew under that storm cloud. This indicates that she has been socialized to the rules and is struggling internally. Evidently she's uncomfortable about the contrast between "how I'm supposed to behave" and "how I behaved." And she has developed enough empathy to notice (and take responsibility for) how she has made Lucia feel. If you go easy, and you ask curious, non-accusatory questions, she will probably open up about what she did. Once these feelings are on the table, I would suggest you validate her discomfort: "You seem upset about hitting Lucia. I'm glad you know that wasn't the right thing to do." By helping her surface her interior distress, and acknowledging that she really does "know better," you set the stage for her to make amends. She may or may not be ready for this step, so use a light touch: "Do you know what people can do when they are sorry they hurt someone else?"

Here's where your everyday behavior comes into play. You are, of course, a role model. If you have created a home where people openly apologize and even forgive, your child will have a rich memory bank of "what people can do when they are sorry." More about that later in this section.

Now, back to the child you are coaching — and by coaching, I mean guiding, not directing. If Alison knows exactly what she wants and needs to do, she might run right over to Lucia and say she's sorry. Or you might need to help her figure out what she's going to say and to rehearse it. A shy child may even need you to speak for her (thus modeling an apology) the first few times: "Lucia, Alison wants me to tell you she is sorry she hit you." However, before you step in, be very sure that she is actually feeling remorseful and that she really wants you to state the apology for her. Otherwise, it's just a forced apology-by-proxy.

I can just about promise you that Lucia will be OK with this. In my experience, kids are much more forgiving and less "grudgy" than adults. Lucia may be cheered by the apology and ready to resume business as usual without explicitly accepting the apology. Little kids (like a lot of adults) tend to show forgiveness not by word but by deed. If you see a positive response from her but you don't hear her say "It's OK" or something indicating forgiveness, you could reassure your child: "It looks like Lucia is happy you apologized to her. Now both of you are feeling friendly again."

Lots of parents insist that their children apologize for transgressions as soon as the kids can speak, long before they could possibly have any feelings of remorse. I suggest to parents that forcing a child to say "I'm sorry" *when he is not sorry* could be seen as teaching hypocrisy. And I think insisting that the wronged child (who may still be grouchy and not ready to move on) submit to a hug or handshake in a charade of forgiveness is plain silly. But my bigger concern is that having to do a lot of ritualized, meaningless apologizing before empathy actually kicks in — and with it, the capacity for feeling remorse — might short-circuit a child's development of genuine fellow-feeling.

Why would forced apologies stunt his emotional growth in this way? Because the child who is made to apologize is deprived of what apologizing is all about! Apologizing is a *process*, one that can be facilitated, as described above, with gentle coaching. It starts on the inside:

- I become aware that I have hurt someone's body or feelings
- Spontaneously and independently, I feel remorse about that
- This makes me feel awful — disconnected from my better self
- I wonder what I can do to make things right
- I think about what my role models (parents, older siblings) do when they feel remorseful
- I apologize
- [Perhaps I am forgiven]
- I feel better — unburdened, reconnected to a "me" that I can feel good about
- I can see that the other person feels better too, released from the weight of resentment

Kids can feel the difference between a genuine process and just getting their card punched. We've all seen a child "fauxpologize" with that aggrieved sigh, that indifferent shrug or roll of the eyes. A forced apology, a coerced pardon simply do not — cannot — work the magic. By having a meaningless ritual stand in for the real thing, I think we dilute its meaning and power. When we cheapen the value of apology, we may be foreclosing on any likelihood that the ritual will take on meaning later.

In *Parenting from the Inside Out*, Hartzell and Siegel show us that one of the recurring themes in the family drama is "rupture and repair." People in relationships inevitably hurt one another from time to time, but they experience remorse and they can make amends. Do your kids see adults apologize and forgive? It's a powerful idea. We have to remember that they have no innate way of knowing what to do when they've hurt someone. They really haven't got a clue. Although it may feel stagey or awkward at the beginning, modeling is the easiest way to teach them the simple beauty of repairing a rupture. Imagine the impact on a child of hearing an unpleasant argument between his parents at night and then bearing witness to this scene the following morning at breakfast:

Mom: Honey, I'm sorry I was grouchy last night. I said some awful things.

Dad: I forgive you. You must have had a horrible day at work. (They hug.)

What does the child learn from this simple exchange? To answer that question, we have to look at how kids react to rupture. Even when kids can't make meaning of what's going on, they have great antennae for detecting strong negative feelings. They are really good at taking the emotional temperature of a room — or a household. Kids are upset by heated arguing, and they experience anxiety in its chilly aftermath. Observing the brief apology/forgiveness scenario above, the child gets to partake of emotional closure along with her mom and dad. She learns that rupture can be repaired, and she's provided with a model of what that looks like. She sees with her own eyes (and senses with those great antennae) how *freeing* it is to apologize and to forgive: the wrongdoer is released from aching remorse and the wronged person can shed that resentment and bitterness. She learns that apologizing makes you bigger, not smaller. And so does forgiveness.

She also learns that a person's integrity is restored through the repair of a rupture. After all, integrity means *wholeness* as well as *moral decency*. Wrongdoing means your worse self has taken leave of your better self — so when we have wronged someone, we feel splintered, detached from the self we feel proud of. The wronged person, too, experiences resentment as distracting and depleting. Both self-recrimination and rancor damage our personhood. Reconciliation puts both parties back together again. Let's consider the following questions.

**What about when a parent wrongs a child?** Understandably, the parent is anxious about revisiting a crazy moment. It's tempting to bury it, or try to whitewash or spin it. But what happened *happened* and both parent and child know this. An unvarnished, heartfelt apology is the best medicine. Siegel and Hartzell point out that parents are sometimes reluctant to apologize to their children for fear of losing face. What's important to keep in mind is that regrettable parent behavior — what they call "taking the low road" — is what actually makes us lose face. Apologizing is not a defeat. It's an opportunity to reclaim your better self, which *restores* face. Making amends, by repairing the rupture, makes us whole again, both in our own eyes and in the eyes of our child.

**Should you be apologizing more, or does your apology style need a tune-up?** For starters, try to steer clear of saying "I'm sorry, but — " and then unleashing a string of self-justifications. An unqualified apology is a thing of beauty.

**Do you try to take shelter behind the passive voice?** Saying "Bad decisions were made" is an attempt to distance yourself from the bad decisions you made. Your listener probably knows the decisions were yours. That person will likely respect you more if you own the mistake, apologize directly for it, and move on.

**Do you say "I'm sorry *if* I hurt your feelings"?** This conveys some doubt as to whether you are to blame and whether the person has a right to feel hurt. Try taking the person's word for it that they were upset by what you said or did, and say simply, "I'm sorry I hurt your feelings." If you need to be extra-clear, you can say, "I'm sorry I hurt your feelings. It wasn't intentional." This lets them know that even though you didn't mean to hurt them, you acknowledge the hurt, and you take responsibility for having caused it.

Trust the power of apology. It can accomplish great things. It can restore your sense of well-being by off-loading what is heavy, worrisome and painful. Retaking the high road boosts your self-worth and reconnects you to your better self.

**And what about when someone apologizes to you?** You might want to do a little cost/benefit analysis of that grudge you're nursing: *How much is this resentment bringing me down?* versus *What am I getting out of it?* Holding a grudge has been described as allowing someone you dislike to live in your brain rent-free. But I don't think anyone has spoken about it as eloquently as Desmond Tutu — who certainly knows a thing or two about forgiveness! — so I will leave it in his capable hands:

---

To forgive is not just to be altruistic. It is the best form of self-interest. It is also a process that does not exclude hatred and anger. These emotions are all part of being human. You should never hate yourself for hating others who do terrible things: the depth of your love is shown by the extent of your anger.

However, when I talk of forgiveness I mean the belief that you can come out the other side a better person. A better person than the one being consumed by anger and hatred. Remaining in that state locks you in a state of victimhood, making you almost dependent on the perpetrator. If you can find it in yourself to forgive then you are no longer chained to the perpetrator.

---

When someone apologizes to you, there is a power shift. Before the apology, you had the moral high ground but you felt diminished in power. Now the other person has seized the moral high ground, but the power to release him or her rests with you. It's tempting to hold on tight to that power. The next move is up to you, and you have options:

- Acknowledgment ("Thank you")
- Acceptance ("I accept your apology")

- Forgiveness ("I forgive you")

Think about how far you want to go. You probably know which option will make the apologizer feel best, but which one will bring *you* the most satisfaction and release? Just as the wrongdoer's burden is remorse, the wronged person's burden is resentment. As the person who has been wronged, how can you best set down *your* burden?

The moral high ground is not exclusive real estate — there's room up there for everyone! When we ought to apologize, or when someone apologizes to us, providing us with an opportunity to forgive, we need to remember that our children are watching — and learning.

In this chapter, I shared a number of ideas for enhancing relationship talk 24/7. What it boils down to is that the easiest way to teach a behavior is to do it. Talking about feelings, using I-messages and active listening, reframing insults, avoiding shame, and waiting for empathy to kick in before *gently* addressing sharing and apologizing — these are all ways to model respectful, effective communication. They are more than just techniques that make mediation easier. They are guidelines that make life with other people — and your family, where it all starts — truer and more meaningful.

# 10

# CONCLUSION

*P*eace is such hard work it should be a verb! For a parent, it takes much more effort to mediate than to arbitrate. And it takes more time. When we think of peace in the family, what usually comes to mind is that afternoon at the park or that day at the beach when, miraculously, there was no arguing or conflict. That idea of peace truly feels like quality family time! What a delicious memory to savor. It's like a great snapshot — a happy accident of time and place. That's peace in the sense of the absence of conflict. And it's so very rare.

When we're hanging out with our kids and conflict rears its head, we want to treat it as an unwelcome stranger and slam the door on it. After all, it intrudes on our quality time with our kids, right? We could shut it down by means of a quick decision or distraction. But if we accept conflict as commonplace and natural instead of intrusive, the better prepared we are to meet it head-on. Mediating can be constructive, engaging, creative, enlightening, and emotionally rich. If that's not quality time, I honestly don't know what is.

The most compelling description I ever heard of peace-as-a-verb was this: my friend and colleague Patti Cunha, who co-directed Oakdale School, said, "peace is a garden." An avid gardener, Patti knows what she's talking about. I'm so grateful for this metaphor. Like gardening, making peace is serious, grubby, challenging work. Like gardening, it provides satisfaction and yields long-reaching rewards. And like gardening, it's never done.

Let's imagine you spend the day working in a garden. You harvest vegetables, pull weeds, haul dirt, dig holes, sow seeds, move plants, tidy flower beds, and sprinkle water. Afterward, you shower and make yourself a big glass of iced tea. You plop down in a comfortable chair and enjoy the vista — an inviting, well-groomed, lovely-hued garden. Which of these activities is gardening — the day's work or the late-afternoon interlude? It's the work, of course.

Once again, I encourage you to think of peace not just as the absence of conflict, rather as *the work of dealing with conflict*. I also encourage you to think about the impact mediation can have on your child and the community.

Conflict is here to stay, but peaceful conflict resolution builds character, promotes harmonious relationships, and makes the world a better place. To appreciate this, all you have to do is recall a special friend, roommate, co-worker, neighbor, team member, boss or romantic partner who recognized relational tension and addressed it in a respectful and timely way. This is someone who came to you early in a conflict to talk things out, and who received your overtures at resolution with grace, optimism, and a goodwill effort. When you mediate your children's disputes, you are in fact guiding your child toward becoming that kind of person. I can think of no higher calling than raising conflict-competent kids. What excellent friends, roommates, colleagues, spouses, parents, community members, and citizens of the world they will be!

I don't believe it's overstating the case to say that if you can equip your children with the tools to resolve conflict skillfully, you will advance the cause of peace in a concrete and powerful way. You have my admiration and support. You are a peacemaker.

# ACKNOWLEDGMENTS

This book has been a long time coming. So many friends, relatives and colleagues live within its pages!

In the world of child development, my first big influence was Pacific Oaks, where my children (along with their lucky mom) began their education. Teachers Renatta Cooper, Louise Derman-Sparks, Cory Gann, Cheryl Greer, Maria Gutierrez, Molly Scudder, Mae Varon, and Mary Worthington inspired me deeply and indelibly. As a parent and a professional, I remain grateful to them.

Magda Gerber (Resources for Infant Educarers) reshaped my thinking about babies and toddlers. It was an honor to be guided by this venerable and outspoken — though delightfully modest — educator. She shared her gift of seeing very young people through new eyes, and her memory has a special place in my heart.

I was privileged to serve as Director of Los Angeles Family School, where I had the pleasure of working with teachers of rare compassion and talent. I humbly thank Elena Adame, Frances Adame, Lourdes Gutierrez, Elizabeth Anne McCullough, Xiomara "Lupe" Mendez, Vardui Minasyan, Molly O'Connor, Vicki Rank, Maryam Rostami, Ginny Tunks, and Kristine Vardanyan for all that they taught me.

I'm lucky to have as my friends a number of therapists who work with children. Consulting with Karen Dudley, Enrico Gnaulati, Clarene Dong Rosten, and Carol Schneider on matters of child development and well-being has been an education. I thank them for their friendship and for helping me grow professionally.

In the mediation world, I've been especially inspired by the writings and teachings of Kenneth Cloke, Jeff Krivis, Barb North, Brook Olsen, and Avis Ridley-Thomas (Dispute Resolution Program, Los Angeles City Attorney's office.)

I am grateful to all the moms and dads in my classes (and by "my classes" I mean those parenting sessions I attended as a young mother as well as those which I have led in the years that followed) who took risks in sharing their deepest concerns. They trusted that what goes on in Parent Ed stays in Parent Ed. This is always a breathtaking leap of faith. Together we all learned that parenting is knotty business, and you can't untangle the knots if you don't let your hair down first!

A big "thank you" goes out to the many schools that have hosted me for workshops as well as ongoing parent education programs. In particular, Patti Cunha and Nancy Hutton offered me a longtime home at Oakdale School. Special thanks are due to Heather Malley (Caterpillar Cottage), a kindred spirit who is fiercely dedicated to what is good for kids and families.

There's no word in English to describe the moms I have leaned on for support and guidance, so I will rely on Spanish: I wish to acknowledge the many *comadres* who have allowed me into the most intimate corners of mothering (and in some cases, grandmothering) while inviting me to do the same. Adrian Becker, Joni Bender, Amie Brin, Christine Colton, Susie Curtiss, Barbara Heitz, Susan Hisserich, Carolina Huete-Lehman, Trudy Israel (who read my manuscript), Toni Kaplan, Mary Jane Mortimer, Terry Porter, Cheryl Revkin (another reader), Pearl Taylor, Barbara Weismann and Martha Wunsch have long comprised my own personal "floating workshop." This has been a treasured resource, transcending time and place. I thank them all.

I must express gratitude to three special people who inspired me to take my work to the next level. Journalist Madeleine Brand edited my two-hour ramble down to a coherent and compelling half-hour podcast. Listening to her product was akin to seeing myself in a very flattering mirror; it cemented my conviction that these ideas about kids and conflict might be useful to parents. And it was Patti Cunha and Katina Shields who first said, almost in unison, "You have a book here." Katina went on to be a reader of my first manuscript, and many of her ideas and edits were adopted.

It has been a joy to work with Robyn Short of GoodMedia Press. Our meeting was pure kismet, and I have been lucky to have such a kind and skillful shepherd for this project.

I must also thank all the nice people at Kaldi who plied me with caffeine, carbs and wacky, eclectic music during this book's long labor and delivery.

And finally, I'm grateful to my family. Thanks go to John Donley for believing in all of this when I was just scribbling ideas on napkins. And to my kids, David North Meadow and Sarah Meadow Walsh — they have taught me so much more than I could ever teach them.

# ABOUT SUSAN NORTH

Photo credit: Tanne Willow

Susan North has been working with children and their families since completing UC Berkeley's Early Childhood Education program in 1971. Her professional experience includes teaching and administration for Head Start, running parent/toddler programs, and directing full-day preschools. She was a Master Teacher with LA Unified's Parent Education Division. More recently, Susie became trained in mediation and facilitation through the L.A. City Attorney's Office Dispute Resolution Program, Ken Cloke's Center for Dispute

Resolution, and Centinela Youth Services. She opened her mediation practice in 2007 and now divides her time doing conflict resolution, parent education, parent coaching, blogging, teaching school-age kids to be peer mediators, and volunteering with Southern California Family Mediation in the Child Dependency Courts.

# ANNOTATED BIBLIOGRAPHY

GENERAL PARENTING BOOKS

Of the many good books that provide overall guidance about child development and parenting, here are six that I think are especially helpful. Please, *please* bring one of these to every baby shower instead of a stuffed animal:

Brazleton, T. Berry. *Touchpoints: The Essential Reference – Your Child's Emotional and Behavioral Development*. Perseus Books, 1992. What would we do without Berry Brazelton? His warmth, wisdom, and sensible advice have educated and reassured generations of parents.

Briggs, Dorothy Corkille. *Your Child's self Esteem*. Broadway Books, 1970. This book remains a wise and useful resource for parents. Briggs believed in being emotionally attuned with children, but she was careful to draw a distinction between empathizing with what a child is going through and rushing in to fix everything. Briggs encourages parents to allow kids to experience consequences in order to develop the competencies that lead to *authentic* confidence. Unfortunately, the so-called "self esteem movement" that got a

foothold in the late sixties has nearly succeeded in giving the term a bad name. It's a shame that misguided people have interpreted "building self esteem" as flooding children with praise and rewards while shielding them from all unpleasant experiences. Kids raised this way become addicted to constant validation, something the world outside their family doesn't provide. Understandably, they often have trouble getting launched and staying motivated, and they struggle to form a realistic self-image. They also lack resiliency; feeling entitled for everything to go well, they crumple or rage when it doesn't. As Briggs wisely counsels, dealing with frustrations and disappointments —
even small failures — is what makes kids strong and flexible. Adults with genuine self-esteem find validation within, and they are resilient enough to roll with the punches.

Davis, Laura and Keyser, Janis. *Becoming the Parent You Want To Be.* Broadway Books, 1997. Davis and Keyser have given us more of a workbook than an instructional manual. Focusing on the first five years, they present nine powerful childrearing themes and offer lots of penetrating questions for parents to ponder together. The authors honor the reader's intelligence and capacity for problem-solving. The title says it all: *this is your journey and you will figure it out.* The book has a detailed, extensive index, which serves the busy, "need to browse'" parent as well as the cover-to-cover reader.

Faber, Adele and Mazlish, Elaine. *How to Talk So Kids Will listen & Listen So Kids Will Talk.* Harper Paperbacks, 1999. This terrific guide to good communication is full of engaging scenarios and cartoons that get right to the heart of things. Beginning with the words, "I was a wonderful parent before I had children," the authors share personal recollections as well as a rich trove of narratives from their parenting classes.

Siegel, Daniel J., M.D., and Hartzell, Mary, M.Ed. *Parenting from the Inside Out.* Penguin, 2004. Writing in a very personal and confiding style, the authors encourage us to dig deep in order to grow and thrive in the parenting role. Siegel and Hartzell back up everything they say with fascinating neuroscientific evidence, and they include exercises for the reader. In this way, the book manages to be at once rigorous and engaging.

Wipfler, Patty and Schore, Tosha, M.A. *Listen: Five Simple Tools to Meet Your Everyday Parenting Challenges*. Hand in Hand Parenting, 2016. This book epitomizes the saying, "It's simple but not easy." The authors teach the power of listening to children by breaking it down into broad thematic chunks. They unpack each theme with lively and touching scenarios.

## BOOKS SPECIFICALLY ABOUT RAISING SIBLINGS

Again, there is a long list of books on the subject of raising siblings. These are some of my favorites:

Ames, Louise Bates with Haber, Carol Chase. *He hit me first: when brothers and sisters fight*. Dembner Books, 1982. This book, produced by the venerable Gesell Institute, begins with an astonishing assertion: siblings fight in order to have something to do and because it amuses them. Bates and Haber have a good eye for spotting this "because it's there" type of squabbling that is really not worth a parent's attention. They believe that spending time over children's arguments is usually a waste of time, shrugging, "Don't be a patsy." For legitimate disputes, they hint at mediation, saying "Try to teach your children the power of words to work out agreements, compromises, contracts." However, they promote what to me are the unhelpful practices of separating children in conflict or simply removing the object they are fighting over. The book presents Gesell-based findings about how siblings get along at different ages and according to birth order. It provides helpful information (and reading suggestions for parent and child) about bringing a new baby into the house. There is also a short, persuasive chapter (11) which puts forth the reasons to have more than one child. Overall, the book reassures parents about the normalcy of sibling conflict — that it can be managed but never eliminated.

Brazleton, T. Berry and Joshua D. Sparrow. *Understanding Sibling Rivalry the Brazelton Way.* Da Capo Press, 2006. An altogether sensible and compassionate guide written in a conversational style, this small book covers everything you could possible want to know about raising siblings. (I could quibble with his ideas about making kids apologize, but I'm in the minority.) Brazelton doesn't sugar-coat the experience of bringing a new baby into the family; he presents scenarios that tug at our emotions and threaten any parent's composure. But he offers practical ideas, including words to use, for handling all the feelings that arise. He is clear that both parents must work in close partnership in order to tag-team effectively. The book is full of great sidebars that distill key elements in a chapter into concise form. These will refresh your memory and help you set an intention. One of the most striking observations Brazelton makes is that *it's extremely unusual for siblings to hurt one another badly unless the parent or another responsible adult is nearby!*

Calladine, Carole and Andrew Calladine. *Raising Brothers and Sisters Without Raising the Roof* (originally titled *Raising Siblings.*) Winston Press, 1983. The authors, who are both family counselors and the parents of four kids, have interesting things to say about the family as a political unit. The Calladines recommend both mediation and arbitration. Parents and kids alike can step in to mediate, but the family also uses a "jury system," in which a disinterested sibling can be recruited to rule on a dispute between two other siblings.

Dunn, Judy. *Sisters and Brothers: The Developing Child.* Harvard University Press, 1985. This exploration of siblinghood is rich with dialogues and scenarios that are as funny, poignant and cringe-inducing as they are real. The book's three overarching themes are 1) the way siblings influence one another, 2) why some pairs of siblings get along so much better than others, and 3) how siblinghood serves as a window into the individual child's socio-emotional and intellectual development. Written in a fairly academic tone, the book presents an unvarnished and probing look at life with siblings. It could serve as a *"What to Expect When You're Expecting"* for parents awaiting, planning for, or considering a second child. A useful bibliography is included.

Faber, Adele and Elaine Mazlish. *Siblings Without Rivalry: How to Help Your Children Live Together So You Can Live Too.* Avon Books, 1988. Reading this book feels like being part of a great parenting class, with all the informality, coziness and trust which that implies. The authors let their hair down about personal experiences and they include many scenarios and Q&As from their classes. Parent behaviors (both helpful and not-so-helpful) are illustrated in cartoon form, bringing the issues to life simply and effectively. Faber and Mazlish stress that rivalry is normal, and that allowing its expression is what keeps bad feeling from festering and causing damage: "Give children in fantasy what they don't have in reality." (When a child discloses negative feelings about a sibling, it's more powerful — and therapeutic — to acknowledge the feelings rather than deny, rationalize or scold.) The book devotes an entire chapter to dealing with relations between a disabled sibling and a typically developing one. The chapter about dealing with conflict proposes that the parent begin with a process that looks a lot like mediation (helping the kids identify the feelings and the issues) but then suggests the parent leave the room. (I find that this is hard to pull off with very young children and/or when emotions are extremely high.) Later in the book, they propose a family meeting for resolving conflicts the children can't solve independently. This looks more like an actual mediation, though it's not developed in great detail. The book's final chapter, "Making Peace with the Past," offers touching and profound stories of parents who grapple with memories of rivalry from their own childhoods. Reading these stories promotes self-inquiry and provides the kind of insight that might help a parent raise siblings more skillfully.

Friedman, Joan A., Ph.D. *Emotionally Healthy Twins: A new philosophy for Parenting Two Unique Children.* Da Capo Press, 2008. The author, who herself is a twin and who raised a pair of twins along with three other children, has very interesting things to say about being a twin and raising twins. She unpacks the "twin mystique" and offers myriad ways to avoid this trap. In a time when we are seeing multiple births more often than ever, this book is a necessary and encouraging guide.

Goldenthal, Peter. *Beyond Sibling Rivalry: How to Help Your Children Become Cooperative, Caring and Compassionate.* Holt Paperbacks, 2000. Whereas a lot of books about siblings spotlight rivalry as an existing condition, this book's focus is largely preventive. Dr. Goldenthal presents rich and varied scenarios, indicating how parents can lay down a healthy foundation for siblinghood. His views on fairness, generosity and differences are particularly thoughtful and worthwhile. Goldenthal urges us to look deeply into our own personal histories for an understanding about how we've been influenced, for better and for worse, by our family of origin. He encourages us to deploy these insights in order to hone our parenting skills, saying, "the more we can do to straighten out our own lives and to sort through our own baggage, the lighter the load will be for our children." He de-mystifies family therapy, pulling no punches with his list of red flags indicating the need for intervention. And he walks us through the steps for getting help. Goldenthal includes a useful appendix for parents seeking professional help with extreme cases of sibling rivalry.

Hart, Sybil. *Preventing Sibling Rivalry: Six Strategies to Build a Jealousy-Free Home.* Free Press, 2001. Despite a title that overpromises, this book explores jealousy in a straightforward and enlightening way. Hart begins with some myth-busting, then goes on to discuss the mother's and father's roles. She has surprising things to say — for example, that parents can be ambivalent when an older sibling acts out towards the baby. (A jealous outburst can be experienced by the parent as upsetting and yet oddly flattering.) Hart's suggestion that parents replicate (at home) her test for "jealousy temperament" which she has developed in a research setting strikes me as problematical. My first concern is that findings in reliable clinical studies are "smoothed out" by virtue of the fact that many, many test subjects are used. To run a test on one's own child at home can result in misleading conclusions skewed by mood, overall health, time of day, and any number of variables. A second concern is that believing one's toddler or preschooler to be extremely jealous in disposition might cause undue stress and worry to expectant parents, or become a self-fulfilling prophesy. It will be what it will be! That said, Hart's other five strategies for diffusing and managing jealousy are sound.

Levitt, Jo Ann, M.A., R.N., Levitt, Marjory, Ph.D., and Levitt, Joel. *Sibling Revelry: 8 Steps to Successful Adult Sibling Relationships*. Dell Publishing, 2001. Two sisters and their brother present ideas for repairing and deepening sibling relationships in adulthood. This text has a workbook format, based on the three-day workshops they jointly teach. The work is based on meditation, recollection and journaling. Assuming one could get cooperation with a sibling to participate, I imagine this process could be enormously healing. (The authors recommend using the book even if a sibling is unavailable, through estrangement or death.) It's easy to see how this book could be used to direct the kind of self-study (recommended by Siegel & Hartzell, Goldenthal, and Faber & Mazlish) that clears away any debris of childhood which might impede good parenting — especially good parenting of siblings. The book is poignant in describing troubling degrees of dysfunction as well as people's surprising capacity for repair. It ends with the profound assertion that how we get along with siblings informs our relationship with the world and all the people in it: "Whatever healing and integration comes about among brothers and sisters establishes a feeling of connection through which we begin to sense the whole world as one family."

Markham, Dr. Laura. *Peaceful Parent, Happy Siblings: How to Stop the fighting and Raise Friends for Life*. The Penguin Group, 2015. Great ideas abound in this informative guide. Dr. Markham digs deep into the sibling bond as well as the causes of rivalry. However, one caveat: I'm not entirely comfortable with her ideas about "scheduling a meltdown." While it's perfectly true that an attuned parent can tell when trouble is brewing, and while I have to admit that I'd rather entertain a meltdown in my living room than at the supermarket, it feels manipulative to hasten things in the way she suggests. I think big emotions run their own course and that it's best to simply offer the warmth and empathy she suggests, without any added gimmickry. This sets the stage for kids to experience their feelings in an authentic, organic (albeit sometimes inconvenient) way. Despite this one reservation, I feel the book has much to offer. Unique among sibling books, it details the *unfolding* of sibling rivalry as a developmental process between two continually maturing children. For example, dealing with a new baby feels completely different than what happens when that baby learns to crawl! And Markham is a proponent of mediating sibling disputes from a neutral stance.

Merrell, Susan Scarf. *The Accidental Bond: The Power of Sibling Relationships*. Times Books, 1995. This is an unusual book, both anecdotal and theory-based. Scarf, a journalist, interviews eight sets of siblings at some length and comments about her findings using research and literary references as well as reflections by individual psychologists and therapists. The way Scarf bridges theory and example make this an engrossing, informative read. Early in the book, she identifies "The three C's" of Competition, Cooperation and Comparison. Her assertion is that there are a limited number of sibling themes which prevail in the narratives. A standout section of the book is chapter eight, where Scarf focuses her attention on a pair of siblings one of whom is developmentally disabled. And in chapter nine there is a section where she examines and debunks some of the commonly-held theories of birth order and personality.

Samalin, Nancy. *Loving Each One Best: A Caring and Practical Approach to Raising Siblings*. Bantam, 1997. Samalin wisely observes that a lot of information about sibling conflict is aimed at helping parents understand the children's point of view. Not wanting to duplicate effort, she focuses on the strain sibling rivalry puts on parents. Since this is another book that's workshop-based, reading it feels like participating in a very intimate and skillfully led parenting class: "Most often, the greatest wisdom available to harried parents comes from the mouths of other parents." In Chapter 4, she touches briefly on the parent's role as mediator. Chapter 8 ("Kids Tell Their side of the Story") is a touching and sometimes hilarious collection of kids' candid remarks on siblinghood. Samalin has interesting things to say about what she calls "the Fairness Trap," saying that any attempt to be even-Steven in all things is a losing game. She also points out an interesting paradox: parents uniformly recall all sorts of quarreling from their own childhoods, and yet they wish for (and sometimes even expect) their own children to get along beautifully! She includes a very comprehensive and useful bibliography. Appendix B contains the full text of the questionnaire she used in researching the book. This contains great discussion questions and / or topics for a parent (or a pair of parents) to reflect upon.

# Index

Index

Index

CPSIA information can be obtained
at www.ICGtesting.com
Printed in the USA
FSHW011348070120
65832FS